No Matter the Wreckage
Poems by Sarah Kay

☙

Write Bloody Publishing
America's Independent Press

Austin, TX

WRITEBLOODY.COM

No Matter the Wreckage

Kay, Sarah
First edition
ISBN: 978-1-938912-48-1

Cover art by Anis Mojgani
Proofread by Philip McCaffrey
Edited by Derrick Brown, Cristin O'Keefe Aptowicz, and Jan Kawamura-Kay
Interior illustrations by Sophia Janowitz
Interior layout by Ashley Siebels

Type set in Bergamo from www.theleagueofmoveabletype.com

Printed in Tennessee, USA

Write Bloody Publishing
Austin, TX
Support Independent Presses
writebloody.com

To contact the author, send an email to writebloody@gmail.com

MADE IN THE USA

No Matter the Wreckage

No Matter the Wreckage

I.

II.

III.

IV.

V.

VI.

VII.

VIII.

IX.

I.

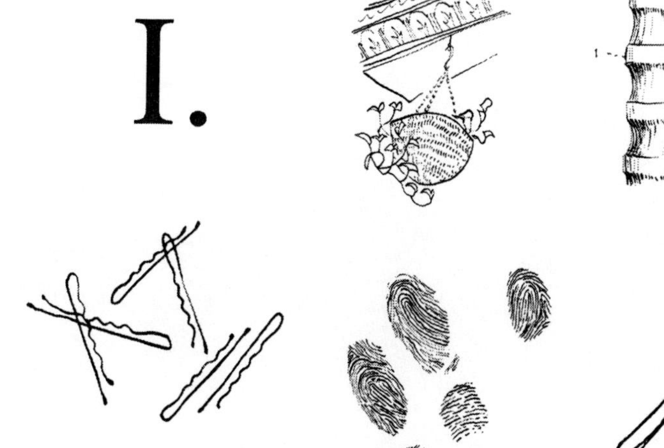

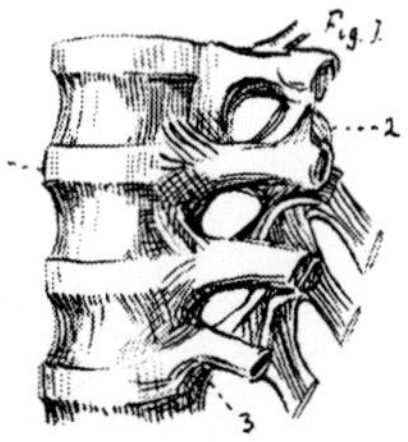

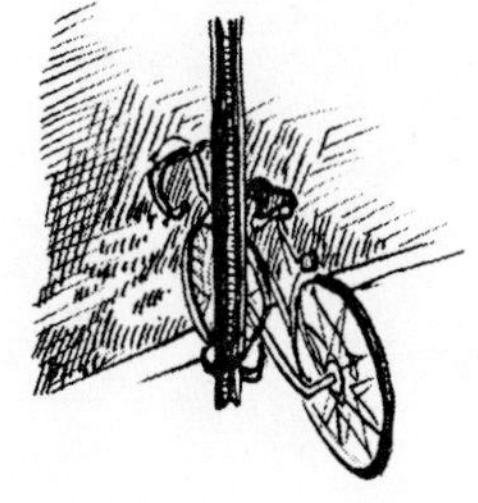

Love Poem #137

I will wake you up early
even though I know you like to stay through the credits.

I will leave pennies in your pockets,
postage stamps of superheroes
in between the pages of your books,
sugar packets on your kitchen counter.
I will Hansel and Gretel you home.

I talk through movies.
Even ones I have never seen before.

I will love you with too many commas,
but never any asterisks.

There will be more sweat than you are used to.
More skin.
More words than are necessary.

My hair in the shower drain,
my smell on your sweaters,
bobby pins all over the window sills.

I make the best sandwiches you've ever tasted.
You'll be in charge of napkins.

I can't do a pull-up.
But I'm great at excuses.

I count broken umbrellas after every thunderstorm,
and I fall asleep repeating the words *thank you*.

I will wake you up early
with my heavy heartbeat.
You will say, *Can't we just sleep in*, and I will say,
No, trust me. You don't want to miss a thing.

Subway

Next time it rains, come with me to 96th and Broadway.
The subway station there has a grate with no roof
and the rainfall slips between the grating up above
and hits the tops of coming trains so that it
flies back up in all directions,
splattering the platform like a painter's palette.

Or else, come with me on a night without rain
and stand with me so that we may peer through
the cracks in the grate and see the soles of New York pass by—
the strips of dark blue evening
streaked above the whir of metal.

Raising a baby in NYC … is like growing an oak tree in a thimble.
—Manhattan Mini Storage Billboard

The Oak Tree Speaks

Do you know how many ways there are to die in this city?
1. Speeding taxicab.
2. Open manhole cover.
3. The man breathing so heavy at the bus stop.

When I was a teenager, the boy I loved would pay a homeless
guy ten bucks to buy him the cheapest bottle in the liquor store.
My love sucked the glass 'til his teeth were marbles. Rolled
himself down the subway stairs, hopped onto the tracks. Waited.

4. Jealous wife.
5. Brooklyn Bridge.
6. Fire escape.

Only once, he let it get so close I screamed. I had never made
that kind of sound before. He turned, his face a prayer wheel
atop his neck, a smile so foreign I could not speak its language.
Like water running in reverse, he spilled himself up to safety.
When the train hurricaned past, the fist of air rattled my branches.

7. Rooftops, all of them.
8. The barroom brawl.
9. The West Side Highway.
10. The wrong street corner.

In New York, when a tree dies, nobody mourns that
it was *cut down in its prime*. Nobody counts the rings,
notifies the loved ones. There are other trees.
We can always squeeze in one more. Mind the tourists.
It's a nice place to visit, but I wouldn't wanna live there.

11. Disgruntled coworker.
12. Central Park after dark.

13. Backpack through the metal detector.
14.
15.
16.

For years, we wouldn't watch movies where they destroyed New York. *The aliens never take Kansas*, we joked. *They go straight for the heart.* Poor Kansas. All cornfields and skyworks. All apple pie. Nobody to notice if it's missing. Just all that open space to grow in.

The Toothbrush to the Bicycle Tire

They told me that I was meant for the cleaner life;
that you would drag me through the mud.

They said that you would tread all over me,
that they could see right through you,

that you were full of hot air;
that I would always be chasing,

always watching you disappear after sleeker models—
that it would be a vicious cycle.

But I know better. I know about your rough edges
and I have seen your perfect curves.

I will fit into whatever spaces you let me.
If loving you means getting dirty, bring on the grime.

I will leave this porcelain home behind. I'm used to
twice-a-day relationships, but with you I'll take all the time.

And I know we live in different worlds, and we're always really busy,
but in my dreams you spin around me so fast, I always wake up dizzy.

So maybe one day you'll grow tired of the road
and roll on back to me.

And when I blink my eyes into morning,
your smile will be the only one I see.

New York, June 2009

1. The man loading mannequins into the back of a truck in the rain.

There are sirens somewhere uptown, and the
mannequins' hollow necks are becoming teacups for rainwater.
He is holding her around the waist, rolling her down the sidewalk.
The rain is not letting up, and he hurries,
trying not to topple the hourglass.

They stand patiently on the curb while he lifts them
one by one onto the truck bed,
the dirty leather of his palms like gentle tiger paws.

And despite the rain, they do not slump,
but stand tall like dancers:
their perfect postures reminding him
of so many places he would rather be.

2. The man sitting on the fire hydrant at 39th and 8th.

You are not old enough to be my grandfather,
your wrinkles tucked neatly into your plaid collared shirt.
Your face offered upwards, eyes closed.
You are collecting sun rays to take back with you
into the air conditioning.

You are as still as a gargoyle, as frail as a praying mantis.
The traffic and passersby are just whispers in the folds of your ears.
Someone honks, and you breathe in,
the sun baking you like a croissant in the midday light.

3. The last time I apologized.

It was warm and I did not need a sweatshirt.
We stopped in the middle of the block,
a woman with a stroller pushed a pink bundle past us.
You planted your feet firmly when I said your name.
A truck on the street rolled over a grate,
and the metal clanging filled the air like
a speech bubble between our faces.

My fingers found my elbows, my neck bone, the hem of my pants.
Down the block, a man in a dirty apron came outside for a smoke,
wiped his hands on his lap and lit a cigarette,
calling over his shoulder, *Sí, claro. Pero un momento por favor.*

The First Poem in the Imaginary Book

If it were me, when the book arrives,
I would immediately start scanning
pages to find any trace of me.
My name, references to my body,
my secrets, moments we shared.
I would pretend to be horrified if I
found evidence of myself, but really
I would pray to find even a single
mention. You may do nothing like that.
You may not even crack the spine.
You may place this on the bookshelf,
or worse, under a stack of papers.
You may forget it and regift it later
to someone as a Secret Santa.
I will never know.
But just in case you *are* like me,
just in case you do still think about
the way your hands used to piano-key
my spine, the way you would whisper
spells into my ears when I was napping,
the way I slipped notes into your
jacket pockets; just in case you wonder
if all those winks ever meant anything
at all, I will tell you.
You do not need to look very
hard to find your shadow here.
Your fingerprints are on these pages.
So many of your footsteps in the snow.

Mrs. Ribeiro

I was visiting a school in Northern India when I heard it
for the first time in ages. It was barely audible above the shouting
of children—the squeals and laughter bubbling from the schoolyard
through the classroom windows. But it was there: the swish of silk
saris and the jingle jangle of bangles on thin wrists like wind chimes.
This is what learning sounds like. I remember.

When I was five years old, the principal of my Junior School was
Mrs. Ribeiro. She was an Indian woman the size of a nightlight,
and she glided like a sailboat through the hallways of my school.
Once, when I got close enough to grab a fistful of her draping
silk sari, I lifted it to try and see whether she had any feet at all.
I thought she floated.

We begged to be sent to her office: the hanging plants like a jungle
above our heads, her quiet laughter. Adults needed appointments,
but we did not. And even when she was in a grown-up meeting,
all it took was a gentle knock on the door, a peek around the corner,
and she was off calling, *Sorry dear. We'll have to reschedule.*
I have to see someone else about a very important matter.

It's about a gold star. It's about a new diorama.
It's about a finished reading book one level higher than last time.
She visited every classroom, knew every student by name.
She spoke to us like we were scholars. Artists. Scientists. Athletes.
Musicians. And we were. My world was the size of a crayon box,
and it took every color to draw her.

Once, on a New York City sidewalk, a group of women
in brightly colored saris walked by and someone shouted,
Look, Mom. Look at all those principals!
My world was the size of a classroom. It was as tall as I could stretch
my fingers, calling, *Please! Let me be the one to read to Mrs. Ribeiro.*
Let me be the one to show her what I know.

Clothes.
Shirt. Pants. Socks. Shoes.

Animals.
Cat. Dog. Bird. Fish.

Look how much I know.

She brought us guests and artists and a petting zoo.
They set up the cages in the parking lot
while we were still tucked up in our classrooms, unaware.
Rabbits and guinea pigs poked out their noses,
but Mrs. Ribeiro came to rest in front of the llama cage.
She and the llama considered each other for a long time.

She asked if he was tame enough to go inside.
The trainers laughed and told her he was plenty tame,
but he didn't know how to go up stairs.
So she led him to the elevator. And when the doors slid open
on the second floor, there stood Mrs. Ribeiro in her bright pink sari,
with golden bangles and a llama on a leash.

She floated from class to class, and we stared,
cheered, laughed, and shouted.
We tugged at her sari calling,
Miss, what is that? Where did it come from?
She made us wonder. She made us question.
She made us proud of what we had learned.

Clothes.
Shirts. Pants. Shoes. Socks. Saris.

Animals.
Cat. Dog. Bird. Fish. Llama.

Look how much I've learned.

She taught us to share. She taught us to listen
when someone else is speaking.
And then she let us go.

We were dandelion seeds released to the wind,
she asked for no return.
We are saplings now. With gentle hands.

The girl with bright cheeks and messy hairpins
now works at an orphanage in Cameroon. The boy with
the color-ordered markers is now a graphic designer in Chicago.
The one with the best diorama is now an animal activist
in Argentina. The girl who loved to read out loud
is now a poet in India. She let us fly.

So I find myself at the front of a classroom.
My students tug at my sleeves and ask me,
Miss, do all poets have crazy hair and big black boots?
I pray for patience. For wisdom. To find a way to tame all the
peculiar animals of this world, to coax them enough to brave the
elevator, to see the doors slide open to my students' gaping mouths.

All their wild wonder.
They worry about everything.
They worry about what to write.
They worry about their grades.
They worry about who likes whom.
They talk over one another until I cannot hear them.

I tell them, *Listen.* Listen to one another like you know
you are scholars. Artists. Scientists. Athletes. Musicians.
Like you know you will be the ones to shape this world.
Show me how many colors you know how to draw with.
Show me how proud you are of what you have learned.
And I promise I will do the same.

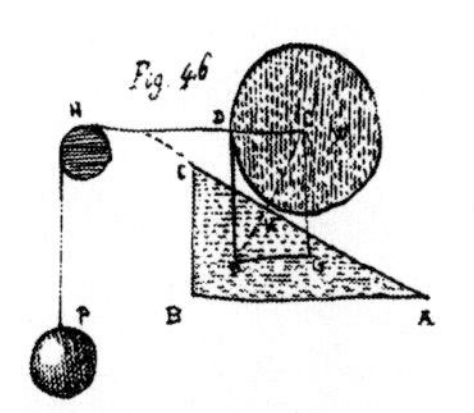

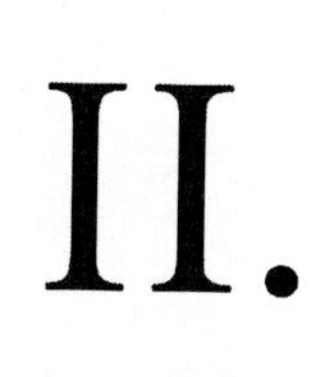

II.

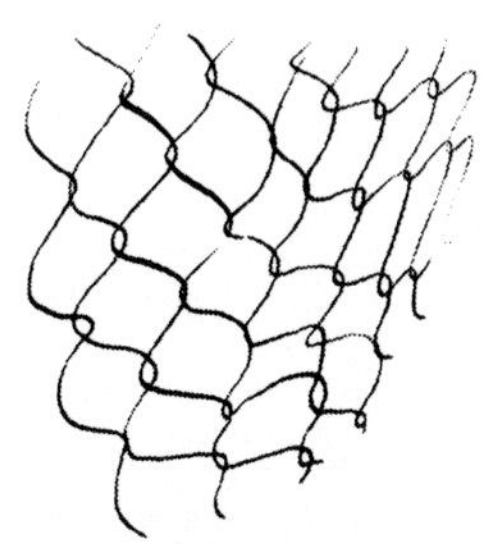

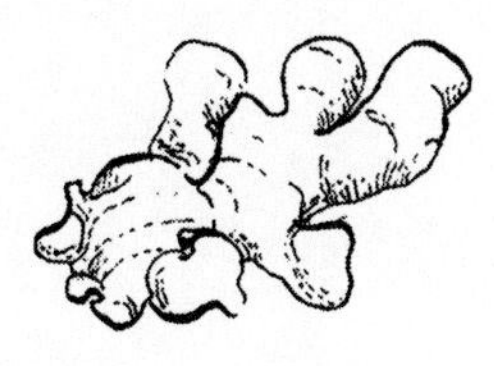

MONTAUK

I am a city girl to my core. The first time my parents took me outside of New York City to visit my uncle in New Jersey, I was standing on the front porch of his lovely suburban home when a fast-moving shadow caused my three-year-old heart to damn near beat out of my chest, and I shouted, *That's the biggest rat I've ever seen.* My uncle calmly responded, *That's a cat, sweetie.* And I shot back, *Oh yeah? Well what's it doing outside then?*

My parents figured there were some things you just couldn't learn from New York City. So every summer we migrated to Montauk, Long Island—the easternmost part of New York State. My father only got two weeks off from work a year, so whenever August rolled around, we packed everything we could into the company van and followed that yellow spotted line of highway out until we couldn't go any farther.

This is where I learned to swim, where I heard the word *shit* for the first time from a bunch of surfers down at the beach. This is where I learned to ride a bike, swerving around puddles on rainy afternoons. This is where I learned to drive a car in the hardware store parking lot; how to kiss a boy with sand between my toes.

Time goes to Montauk to take a break. It loosens its belt, takes a seat on the front porch next to my father and his Weber grill. It putters around the kitchen with my mother while she kneads her homemade sourdough bread, and chuckles when it catches her speaking out loud to herself—telling nobody in particular—*We should roast some peaches tonight. I'll bet oatmeal would be delicious for breakfast tomorrow if we roasted some peaches tonight.*

Time stalls in Montauk. I am seven years old. My little brother is three. He splashes in a baby pool, while I brave the full-length Olympic-sized one by myself. Chubby in my one-piece, my thighs brush against each other as I tread water in the shallow end. I look up and see an older girl: perfect in her bikini, tall, and tan, and probably on her way to meet her handsome Prince Charming boyfriend.

She glows as she glides past me, tosses her hair like she has all the answers, and I wonder if I will ever be a woman like that. That summer, I learn how to wish on stars.

I am twelve years old. My little brother is eight. He can surf better than I can, and I hate it. I wait until he and all the other surfers are done for the day before paddling my fat sponge of a board out past the breakers. There is nobody left in the water. The setting sun makes the ocean glow golden. I tuck my legs up. That summer, I learn how to be alone.

I am sixteen. My brother is twelve and at the beach. I am reading magazines on the couch when my mother appears in the living room holding her laptop, the only computer in the house. My brother has downloaded his first porn video, and my mother is trying to decide what should be done about it. That night when I go to check my email, I discover she has made a new folder on the desktop and labeled it, *PK's Porn*. That summer, I learn how to love my parents.

There are some things you cannot learn in New York City. There are places where fishnets do not mean stockings, where the learning happens in between moments, like after a wave passes, and you break the surface gasping for air.

I am twenty-two. The landmarks are the same. The same stretch of beach, same hardware store parking lot. Some of the names have changed. The pool hasn't. I make my way to the shallow end and wade in slow. In Montauk, I can take my time. I look up to see a little girl, chubby in her one-piece, gripping the wall and watching me enter the water, her eyes the size of summer tomatoes and just as red from all the chlorine-rubbing. I almost speak to her. But before I can, there is a splash behind me. A woman well into her fifties—chubby in her one-piece—has cannonballed into the deep end. She comes up coughing, flailing, water in her nose. She comes up laughing. The little girl giggles. And me? Well, I am laughing, too.

My Parents on Their Way Home from a Wedding

When they pick up the phone,
all I can hear is Simon and Garfunkel
blaring in the background. For a few
seconds, it is only this: wind static
and the strum of guitars, the simple
harmonies of open windows and streaked sunlight.
Then my father's barrel-bass chocolate growl,
my mother's piccolo-breath,
they are laughing through the speaker phone,
telling me about the ceremony, how lovely it was.

There are trees sliding into one another, faster
than they have time to count. *So many flowers,*
they say. *What a beautiful dress.* I was calling
to tell them about something sour, something
less blossom and more thorn, but I inhale;
swallow. It can wait. They are laughing through
the speaker phone, they are laughing, and they
are driving on a highway they have not been on before.

My mother says, *Oops, I think we've gotten lost!*
We might have to call you back. They forget that
I am on the line, point out street corners that
are named the wrong names, notice trees they
could have sworn they passed sometime before.

SLIVERS

When we were three,
Sophia and I were taken
to the beach in Hither Hills.

A seagull came and stole our
bagels, the sand was awful hot,
but the water was perfect on

our warm bellies. Fathers lifted
us high into the air and we squealed,
mothers looked out from under

the beach umbrellas. We went
for a walk on the wooden pier
and both wound up with splinters

in our left feet. Matching splinters!
Matching bathing suits! Matching
wails as fathers propped us up on

the hood of the station wagon,
mothers found the tweezers
in the first aid kit, took turns

alternating between holding ice cubes,
wrestling our wriggling,
and digging out the culprits.

I don't think I actually remember
this day. I don't think the scene
in my head is real—it must instead

be the retelling of the story that
I have memorized and rehearsed—
that my mind has filled in the gaps.

And yet, it would explain why,
twenty-one years later, we
can feel the phantom hurt inside

each other; how our pains align
themselves in symmetry, or in
complement, like mirror selves.

How—when the phone rings,
your voice on the other end
allows me to release my wail,

reach out to squeeze your hand.
We dig the slivers from ourselves
as best we can. When the

hurt remains, you, dearest friend,
will recognize my limp. You will
whimper with me, fully. You will

return with me to the hot sand,
to the menacing gulls, to the water
sweeping us into new and better days.

Brother

You jaywalked your way out of the womb.
I would recognize you anywhere
by the hiccup in your swagger. Tell me,
where in the world did you find all that thunder?

There have never been any seat belts on your side of the car.
You have always known the better magic tricks.
You told me once that I was just the *first draft,*
and I'm inclined to believe you, but you came
with a lot more pieces to assemble and
Mom and Dad never got the manual.

Your compass always points north.
But it's a bit of a crapshoot as to whether or not
you'll ever walk in that direction. I like that.
It keeps people on their toes.

On the merry-go-round of your life, the carousel ponies
are all narwhals. Their horns point straight up.
The day they build you a constellation, it will be
the entire F Train spread across the Milky Way.
You will be a satellite that dips in and out of every car
the moment the train comes to a stop, pissing off
everybody on the subway platform, and kicking up
stardust in your wake. You can solve a *Law & Order*
episode before the first commercial break.

Once, when you were seven, you came into the kitchen
and asked Mom, *Does my name begin with the letter P*
because P is the sixteenth letter of the alphabet and
I was born on June sixteenth, and is Sarah just Sarah because
S is the nineteenth letter of the alphabet and
she was born on the nineteenth day of June?
And when Mom said no, you nodded your head
and left the room mumbling to yourself,
Okay. Just salt and pepper then.

You are my favorite stick of dynamite.
You are the opposite of a rubber band.
There are so many things I would tell you
if I thought that you would listen
and so many more you would tell me
if you believed I would understand.

I hope you know that you were never meant to wear my shadow.
In fact, I'm the one who always steals your shoes.
But is that my sweatshirt you're wearing? It's okay, you can keep it.
I won't tell your secret. In fact, it really does look better on you.

HANDS

People used to tell me that I had beautiful hands.
They told me so often, in fact, that one day I started to
believe them; I started listening. Until I asked my
photographer father, *Hey Daddy, could I be a hand model?*

To which Dad laughed and said, *No way.*
I don't remember the reason he gave,
and it probably didn't matter anyway.
I would have been upset, but there were

far too many crayons to grab, too many
stuffed animals to hold, too many ponytails to tie,
too many homework assignments to write,
too many boys to wave at, too many years to grow.

We used to have a game, my dad and I, about holding hands.
We held hands everywhere. In the car, on the bus, on the street,
at a movie. And every time, either he or I would whisper a
great big number to the other, pretending that we were

keeping track of how many times we had held hands,
that we were sure this one had to be eight-million,
two-thousand, seven-hundred and fifty-three.
Hands learn. More than minds do.

Hands learn how to hold other hands.
How to grip pencils and mold poetry.
How to memorize computer keys
and telephone buttons in the dark.

How to tickle pianos and grip bicycle handles.
How to dribble a basketball and how to peel apart
pages of Sunday comics that somehow always seem to stick together.
They learn how to touch old people and how to hold babies.

I love hands like I love people. They are the maps and
compasses with which we navigate our way through life,
feeling our way over mountains passed and valleys crossed;
they are our histories.

Some people read palms to tell your future,
I read hands to tell your past.
Each scar marks a story worth telling. Each callused palm,
each cracked knuckle, is a broken bottle, a missed punch,

a rusty nail, years in a factory.
Now, I watch Middle Eastern hands
clenched in Middle Eastern fists.
Pounding against each other like war drums,

each country sees their fists as warriors,
and others as enemies, even if fists alone are only hands.
But this is not a poem about politics; hands are not about politics.
This is a poem about love.

And fingers. Fingers interlocked like a beautiful accordion of flesh
or a zipper of prayer. One time, I grabbed my dad's hand
so that our fingers interlocked perfectly, but he changed his
position, saying, *No, that hand-hold is for your mom.*

Kids high five, sounds of hand-to-hand combat
instead mark camaraderie and teamwork.
Now, grown up, we learn to shake hands.
You need a firm handshake, but not too tight, don't be limp now,

don't drop too soon, but for God's sake don't hold on too long . . .
but . . . hands are not about politics?
When did it become so complicated?
I always thought it simple.

The other day, my dad looked at my hands, as if seeing them
for the first time. And with laughter behind his eyelids,
with all the seriousness a man of his humor could muster, he said,
You've got nice hands. You could've been a hand model.

And before the laughter can escape me,
I shake my head at him,
and squeeze his hand.
Eight-million, two-thousand, seven-hundred and fifty-four.

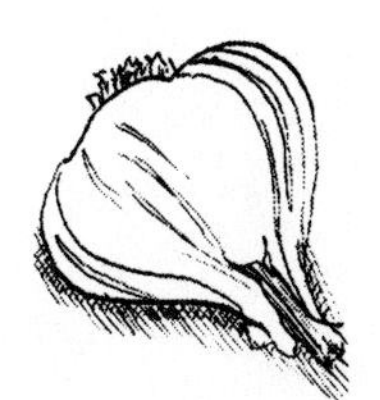

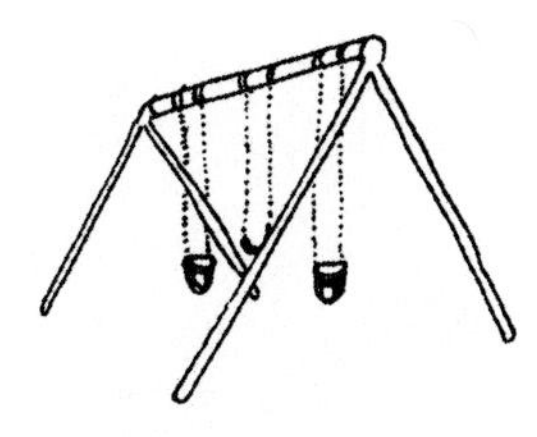

III.

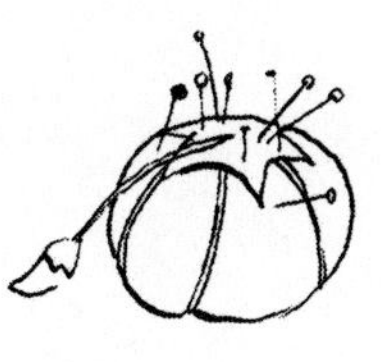

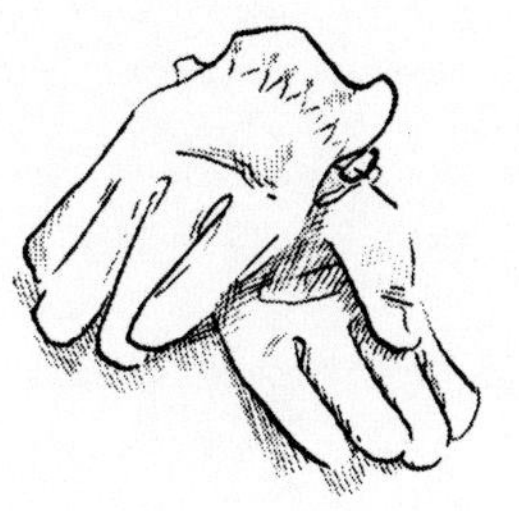

Jellyfish

It was somewhere in between the last day of school and the first, somewhere in between morning and nightfall, somewhere in between New York City and the very tip of Long Island—there was a nine-year-old girl somewhere in between the shoreline and the sand dunes, scanning the horizon like a hawk. Like an Amazon warrior. Like a great cavalry captain. Like Charlemagne on the morning before he took his final enemy: Jellyfish. There were jellyfish on my beach, in my ocean! And that silhouette of a soldier? That was me.

I was the nine-year-old protector. I was the Conqueror of the Jellyfish. I was the Vanquisher of the Venomous. And I was armed. With my plastic bucket and my legs. (Which were strong enough to plant against the pull of the sinking tide, so I could wait until one of those throbbing, red and purple, translucent bubbles of death drifted unsuspecting into the claws of my plastic trap.) And my legs were fast enough to dart back up onto the beach, where I would toss my captives mercilessly into the sand pit I had dug—never stopping for breath! (Only for a juice box, in the cool shade of our green-and-white umbrella.)

I was a man on a mission. Which is to say—girl with a bucket. (But in the bright glare of late August, those two look an awful lot alike.) That bucket was sword and shield. That hole was prison and redemption. There was no repentance. I had no guilt. I was risking life and limb to protect everything I knew to be sacred. And you have to understand: I really believed it was so.

I lost count after twenty-two. The motions became fluid, almost memorized. As day began to sink and pink and orange began to creep their way into the crystal of afternoon sky, seeping like ink into the ocean around my ankles, I grew weary. Mom and Dad called from the beach: Time to turn in my bucket! Time to stop killing the enemy! Time to start thinking about what I wanted for dinner.

And that's when it hit. The one that got away. Quick like lightning, blinding like gunfire, piercing like the point of a spear. I was hit and I was down. I was down hard and fast; it was a hit-and-run. That tentacle was gone before I even had time to register pain. And that pattern lasted all summer long like a railroad track down the back of my hand: a battle scar to mark the war I had fought.

And somewhere in between then and now *irony* slipped its way into my vocabulary. *Laughter* became the antidote for guilt. *Sacrifice* grew to be a Band-Aid for shame. And unnecessary death became the nightmare that rode me piggyback. Somewhere in between then and now I learned that every move you make echoes outwards from your body like ripples on the ocean from a skipping stone. It is what has taught me that Karma is as tangible as the taste of seawater. Somewhere, somebody has a scorecard, so that *eye for an eye, tooth for a tooth* really does come around to bite you in the ass.

What is it about immortality? With the right sword and shield, we think we can fend off anger, fear, and hatred. If our legs are strong enough, we think we can outrun age, loss, and death. That we can always truly live as Master of all the Jellyfish.

Evaporate

Today lasted so long, by the time I arrived at nightfall,
I had forgotten that this morning was this morning.

It seemed so far away, like yesterday, or the day before.
And days and days and days unfolded in the hours between

when first I woke and when now I sit. I notice minutes
move, much more than when I was younger.

Today I looked at my face in a mirror.
I braided my hair. I put on a dress.

Today a child shook my hand like a grown-up
and told me she was in the sixth grade.

It sounded like she said she *wasn't the sick grey*
which made me think that is what she thought I was.

I am watching parts of me evaporate like sidewalk water.
This wet grey, this nighttime dew, gone before morning.

The Ladder

Whenever I hurt myself, my mother says
it is the universe's way of telling me to
slow down. She also tells me to put some
coconut oil on it. It doesn't matter what *it*
is. She often hides stones underneath my
pillow when I come home for the weekend.
The stones are a formula for sweet dreams
and clarity. I dig them out from the sheets,
she tells me what each one is for. My throat
hurts, so she grinds black pepper into a
spoonful of honey, makes me eat the entire
thing. My mother knows how to tie knots
like a ship captain, but doesn't know how
I got that sailor mouth. She falls asleep
in front of the TV only until I turn it off,
shouts, *I was watching that!* The sourdough
she bakes on Fridays is older than I am.
She sneaks it back and forth across the country
when she flies by putting the starter in small
containers next to a bag of carrots.
They think it's ranch dressing, she giggles.
She makes tea by hand. Nettles, slippery elm,
turmeric, cinnamon—my mother is a recipe
for warm throats and belly laughs. Once,
she fell off of a ladder when I was three.
She says all she was worried about was
my face as I watched her fall.

Bricklayer

It is snowing in New York and the Bricklayer's hands are cold.
He should have worn gloves—would have worn gloves
if he had thought there would be a chance of snow—but it is

April for God's sake. Sometimes my father yells so loudly,
he scares himself. Then he has to sit somewhere very still
and very dark to return. Sometimes there is hair in the shower drain,

sometimes the jacket doesn't fit. This hat is itchy, Mother,
and my fingers hurt. Someone has to build this wall. This house,
this family, someone has to place the bricks just so. I will not be

home in time for the holidays. Make sure someone says grace at the
table, make sure someone says thank you. Sometimes my father
wanders room to room in the early hours. He stalks the ghosts

that walk our hallways. The Bricklayer's back is hurting. He bends
into himself like a folding chair, his flannel does not keep out
the snow. This head is itchy, Mother, and my fingers hurt.

Forest Fires

I arrive home from JFK in the rosy hours
to find a new 5-in-1 egg slicer and dicer
on our dining room table.
This is how my father deals with grief.

Three days ago, I was in the Santa Cruz
Redwoods tracing a mountain road
in the back of a pickup truck, watching
clouds unravel into spider webs.

Two days from now, there will be
forest fires, so thick, they will have to
evacuate Santa Cruz. The flames will paint
the evening news a different shade of orange,

and when it happens, I will be in New York City
watching something else on TV. Commercials,
probably, which is all that seems to play
on hospital television sets: the beeping

from the nurses' station mixing with sales jingles—
the theme song for the ailing. My grandmother's tiny body
is a sinking ship on white sheets. I hold her hand
and try to remember open highways.

It really goes to show that it doesn't take
much with these dry conditions to start a fire,
a Cal Fire spokesman will tell CNN on Sunday.
Fire officials have been working tirelessly, but

controlling something this big is impossible.
My mother will point at the celluloid flames,
remind me how lucky I am, how close I had been,
how narrowly I missed this disaster. My father

will point out a commercial for the Brown & Crisp,
repeat line by line how it *bakes, broils, steams,*
fries, and barbeques. He will write down
the number to order it later.

Three days ago, I was barefoot. Balancing
on train tracks, the full moon an unexpected visitor,
the smoke-free air as clean and sharp
as these city lungs could stand.

Two days from now I will find my father
making egg salad in the kitchen, exhausted
after an all-night shift at the hospital. I will
ask if he needs help and understand

when he says no. I will leave him to slice
and dice the things he can. My grandmother
folds her hands on mine and strokes
my knuckles like they are a wild animal she is

trying to tame. She tells me I am gorgeous,
watches a commercial, forgets my name,
tells me I am gorgeous again.
My father watches from the bedside chair,

his mother and daughter strung together
with tightrope hands, fingers that look
like his own. And somewhere in California
a place I once stood is burning.

Poppy

Poppy is four years old. The only shelf in the cabinet she can reach is the one with the plastic Tupperware. She has started filling containers with water, snapping on lids, and placing them about the house. It is her new favorite game. One for Mama, one for Papa, one for Tessa, one for Ollie. Her hands can hold one at a time. Her dress is the color of marmalade, she chirps songs that have no words.

When Poppy is twenty-five, she will follow a love to France. In the summertime she will make jars of cold tea, place them in the sun to steep, forget them in the sunny corners of their house. He will love her for this. That, and the daisies in her hair; the way she reads in doorways, purring show tunes to the crinkle of the page.

When she is forty-seven, Poppy's garden will be the talk of the street. Her French Tulips will dip over the sidewalk, dragging leaves against the pavement. She will carry jugs of water—overflowing onto her arms, her overalls—back and forth from the house to the yard. This is her way now, since her son has worn holes through the garden hose with his trike. She does not mind. He rides circles around the jugs while she sings and turns the soil.

Eighty. And Poppy carries cups of water to leave around the house. One to the desk for while she is writing, one to her bedside every night. The walk to the kitchen is long and her lavender nightgown is thin. *Open the cabinet, find the cup. Turn on the tap, fill it up. Snap on the lid, off to bed.* She hums to the radiator. Sometimes she forgets the words.

Something We Don't Talk About, Part I

One night when it got really bad,
she left right in the middle of dinner.

She got up like she had forgotten
the olive oil but instead she picked

her keys off the rack like a small skeleton
in her hand. She pushed the elevator button

slowly, as though turning off the oven.
She waited for it to reach our floor,

she pulled open the heavy metal door.
She walked in, pressed 1. We watched it happen.

All three of us. The steering wheel of our family
being pulled out through the dashboard.

The slow-motion tire screech.
That empty highway. I remember trying to listen

for the elevator doors closing in the lobby.
PK said, *She took her house keys*, answering

a question nobody had asked.
I didn't tell him that even after a crash,

a key still fits the ignition.
There just isn't anything left to drive.

We kept eating the meal she had made.
I kept listening for a jingle of metal.

But only radio static filled the room,
not a single siren blared. Not even one.

Dragons

My father and brother were born
with cannonball fists. Avalanche tongues.
They know how to light flame to the
smallest injustice. How to erupt into
fireworks from the inside. The silent
anger too. They are capable of keeping
the engine humming, the deep vibration
of fury warm underneath. Me—I was
not born with enough fuel. My anger
often melts into sadness, it will just
disintegrate into shame or fear, my
clenched teeth release into chatter.
But you have found the right mix of
arrogance and alcohol. Place your hands
on me one more time, then again, exhale
the cigarette into my eyes, tell me again
how I'm just not understanding the point,
remind me how you are an expert, touch
my knee, my thigh, my lower back, ignore
me twice, three times, continue talking over
me with the man to my right. There is a
beast in my veins that was birthed by my
father. It is quiet, it sleeps through most
nights. Tonight, sir, my tail twitches in
the darkest caves. Be careful, darling.
Your footsteps land heavy here. Your
racket will wake the dragons.

Hand-Me-Downs

You have taken to wearing around your father's
hand-me-down anger. I wish that you wouldn't.
It's a few sizes too big and everyone can see it doesn't
fit you, hangs loose in all the wrong places,
even if it does match your skin color.

You think you'll grow into it: that your arms
will beef up after all the fighting and it will sit on your
shoulders if only you pin it in the right places with
well-placed conviction.

The bathroom mirror tells you, you look good,
your fists look a lot more justified.
When you dig your hands deep into the pockets,
you'll find stories he left there for you to hand out
to the other boys like car bombs.

On days when everything else is slipping through
your fingers, you can wrap yourself inside of this anger.
This will keep you warm at night, help you drift off to sleep,
with the certainty that no matter what happens,
it will still be there when you wake up.

The longer you wear it, the better it fits.
Until some of those stories are your own. The holes
in the sleeve are from the bullets you dodged yourself.
When it rips, snags on a barbed wire fence or
someone else's family, don't worry.

Your mother and your sister will mend it:
patch the holes, sew the tears, replace a button or two.
They will help you back into it and tell you how proud
they are of you; how good it looks on you. The same way
it looked on your dad and your granddad, too.

And on his father before him and on his father before him.
But back then? Back then there was only sand. Until someone
drew a line. Someone built a wall. Someone threw a stone.

And the crack in the skull that it hit fractured perfectly
like twigs on the branches of a family tree, so someone

threw a stone back. And each fracture, each tiny break
wound itself together into thread. The thread pulled itself
around him, your great-great-great-great-somebody.
And on the other side of the wall, they were knitting just as fast and
theirs fit them just as well, only in a slightly different shade.

So I'm asking, when the time comes, who is going to be
the first to put down the needle and thread?
Who is going to be the first to remember that
their grandfather suffered just as many broken windows,
broken hearts, broken bones? And the first time

you come down to dinner, and your son is sitting at the
dining room table wearing your hatred on his shoulders,
who is going to be the first to tell him it is finally time to take it off?

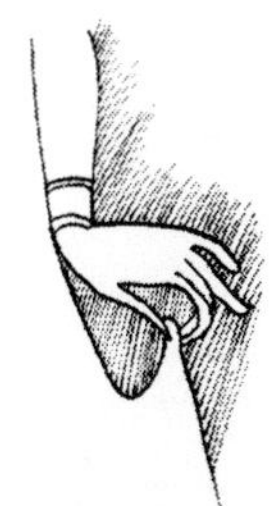

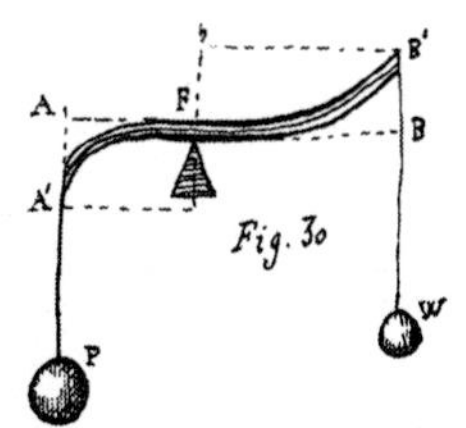

IV.

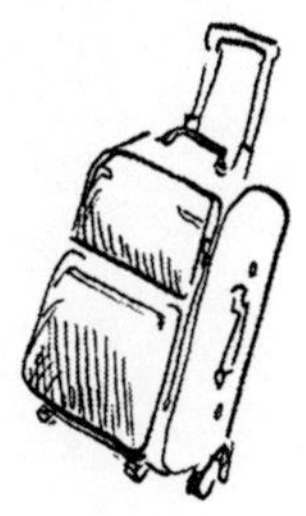

(This poem begins and ends with the song "Shosholoza," a Ndebele folk song that some hail as the "unofficial" or "second" national anthem of South Africa. It was sung by migrant workers in South African mines as a song of resistance and solidarity. The very rough translation is: Moving fast, moving strong, through these mountains like a rolling train to South Africa. You are leaving, you are leaving through these mountains like a rolling train from Zimbabwe.)

Shosholoza

Shosholoza, ku lezontaba stimela siphume South Africa
Wenu yabaleka, ku lezontaba stimela siphume Zimbabwe

Noor Ebrahim had fifty homing pigeons.
He lived in District Six at the center of Cape Town.
Noor Ebrahim lived with fifty pigeons in District Six
at the center of Cape Town, where there were twelve schools
and the Holy Cross Church and the Aspeling Street Mosque
and the Jews on Harrington Street. With the immigrants and
the natives, the Indians and the Malaya,
the Blacks and the Coloureds. Noor Ebrahim lived with fifty pigeons
in District Six at the center of Cape Town, where there was
Beikinstadt Bookstore and Parker's corner shop; where you could
buy bread and paraffin for the stove, fish oil, bulls-eyes
and almond rock; where you could walk to the public baths,
pay a *ticky*, get a fifteen-minute shower, and find yourself between
the gangsters and the businessmen bathing side-by-side, right there,
at the corner of Clifton and Hanover Streets.
Noor Ebrahim lived in District Six at the center of Cape Town.
With fifty pigeons and his family.

Now watch.
Take 1 city: Cape Town.
Divide it into 12 districts.
Now take one of them, District 6,
add 70,000 people over time.
Divide that by the Group Areas Act of 1950
and you wind up with what?

I will give you a hint. It is the same as if you were to divide by race.

So you are left with a remainder of 1 Apartheid Government
and 1 declaration of 1966 which stated that from now on District 6
would be officially recognized as a designated whites-only area.

So, no more Hanover Street with the thick smell of curry
coming from Dout's café, and no more Janjura's groceries,
Maxim's sweeterie, Waynik's school uniforms, and the sound of
children. Shoppers. Merchants. Buses. Laughter. Song. No.
At the end of all that, you are left with only bulldozers.
Leveled buildings. Razed land. Broken glass and brick.
Not even phantoms will haunt this ghost town,
because even their floating figures are not white enough.

Noor Ebrahim moved the ten kilometers to Athlone.
He packed fifty pigeons into their cages and left District Six
at the center of Cape Town. He left the Peninsula Maternity Home
where hundreds of coloured babies were born every year
and the soda fountain where you could sit and watch the ladies bring
their laundry down to the public washhouse three times a week.
He left his house on Caledon Street.
Noor Ebrahim left his home on Caledon Street in District Six
at the heart of Cape Town and moved the ten kilometers to Athlone.

He lived there for weeks, sometimes driving
past the empty pit of land where District Six no longer stood.
The winds blew hard, and they swept through the dust and the dirt
and the broken glass until every blade of grass bent
beneath the weight of what was no longer there.

After three months, the droppings at the bottom of the birdcages
had become three layers thick. Noor Ebrahim decided it was time
to let the pigeons fly free—fly free so they could find their way back.
He knew that not all of them would return that night.
He knew that the next morning, some of those cages
might not be as full. But he also knew that sometimes gravity
can become a little too comfortable.
So that morning, Noor Ebrahim opened the doors on the cages,
and the winds that swept through Cape Town swept through and
lifted all fifty pigeons up into the air in a cloud of feathers, as if to say,

It does not matter how long we have been kept in cages.
It does not matter how strong your gravity is.
We were always meant to fly.

That night, Noor Ebrahim returned from work.
He turned off the car, went around to the back of the house, and cried out in pain. Not a single bird had come back to him.
The cages were lined with droppings and feathers, but no pigeons.
The man who had watched them level his house to the ground without shedding a single tear, now felt his mind go cloudy and his ribcage felt as empty as the ones the birds had abandoned.
He got back into the car to take a drive and clear his mind.

As he drove down the long streets of Cape Town,
the wheel moved beneath his hands and he found himself
on the abandoned roads of District Six.
As he reached Caledon Street, Noor Ebrahim slowed to a stop.
Because there on the empty plot of land where his house once stood, were pigeons. All fifty of them.
Standing amongst the dust and the dirt and the broken glass,
looking up at him as if to say, *Where is our home?*

South Africa. We sing a song of strength.
We go on like a rolling train forever.
We never let gravity become too familiar.
Because we were always meant to fly.

Shosholoza, ku lezontaba stimela siphume South Africa
Wenu yabaleka, ku lezontaba stimela siphume Zimbabwe

India Trio

I.
Outside my window, through the orange drapes,
I can see a light on in the building facing mine.
It is late now, an hour past when well-behaved
citizens will have gone to sleep.
Who finds themselves restless in this
perfect heat? Perhaps it is two people, lying
next to each other on the mattress, sheets
thrown to the ground, knotted on the floor.
It is too hot for lovemaking. Too hot even
for touching. No, I am sure they have both just
been lying there awake, sweating into their
pillows, breathing in the muggy darkness, both
hands placed by their sides, fingers spread
open. They have both been lying still, one
of them desperately trying to fall asleep, the
other measuring the distance between their
fingertips, waiting until the humidity becomes
too wet, the fire on the skin too near; waiting
until this moment to turn on the bedside lamp.
Deciding finally, to honor this kind of arousal
with something other than breath.

II.
Most days, waking is the hardest.
But it is also when Poetry arrives—
stands patiently outside the shower,
places its hands on the mirror,
wipes away the steam.
And then there are days when
sleeping is the hardest. The fight
of muscle against world becomes
so constant, that surrendering
to slumber doesn't promise
nearly enough relief. These are
the times when hands feel nothing

but empty. These are the times
when the ceiling fan is left off.
When this heat becomes the only lover
to hold, the only weight
that feels familiar anymore.

III.

Tonight, I raised my hand to my face
to brush away an untamed curl of hair,
and when it slid past my nose, it smelled
suddenly of you. Not your cologne, or
the soap you use, not shampoo or aftershave.
That skinsmell I find tucked into your
neckplace—that late afternoon nap's shadow
that rises and falls, rises and falls against
my sheets, leaving traces of you in every
pillowcase. I held very still and closed
my eyes, trying to keep whatever particles
of you I managed to steal, until even my
inhale meant losing you. So then I didn't
breathe at all, just held my hand against my
cheek, and for a moment, felt that it was you.

Jetlag

My pendulum has swung so far past its point,
it has gotten wrapped around me, throws
me back and forth from my own neck.

My pupils are the bottoms of exclamation points.
I am so tired I can only come up
with words in small bursts of: *Water.*

Stewardess. Peanuts. Aisle. Magazine.
The turbulence hits and someone has turned
on the washing machine in my skull. The

woman across the aisle has started praying.
I see her mouth: *Please let me get home.*
Please let me get home safe.

How fast does a body fall
when it is not yet in its own time zone?
Where did I leave summer? Is my passport

still strapped to my ribs? How fast can I swim
with a tin can plane tied to my ankle?
Captain. Speaking. Sorry.

Fasten. Seatbelt. Change. Cabin. Pressure.
Please. Home. Please. Home. Safe.
The ground is a letter I mailed days ago.

Someone must have it by now.
What was the last thing I said on the phone?
Was it, *I love you?* Was it, *I'll see you soon?*

Paws

Inspired by Cristin O'Keefe Aptowicz's "Hound"

The third time your plane is delayed,
your voice on the phone has melted to a whimper.

I don't know when we'll take off,
you say. *I'm going back to the desk to ask.*

All day, you have been sending me text messages
of puppy love. *I can't wait to kiss you.*

I miss the nook of your neck. How strange,
that when you are away, I reach for my

cell phone's buzz as if it were your hand.
Each shiver in my pocket, a way to find you.

I will see you soon, Love, this morning's text promised.
And yet now it is night, and you are still lost

in an airport somewhere in Florida, and I am still here,
trying to comfort you through this phone.

I'm okay, you promise. *I just wish I was home.*
You sigh into the speaker. The static crackles.

In November, a doctor put your dog to sleep.
You didn't tell me it had happened for the whole day,

because you didn't want me to worry or be upset.
I didn't find out until your parents told me, and I reached

for your hand, not knowing what else to do.
I have never had a pet, I do not know this kind of loss.

The quiet of your kitchen does not sound empty to me,
I cannot hear the missing padding of paws on tiles,

the missing pant and rumble of her belly. But the first few times
you came home that week, I did see the way you opened

the front door: the extra moment you waited, the way
your shoulders sank. *She was old*, you told me.

*She didn't get around like she used to. She didn't
even jump up when people came in, didn't run to*

*bark and greet me at the door. But she was here.
At least I knew she would be here when I got home.*

Recently, there have been more airports for the both
of us. Different suitcases and baggage claims, different

time zones and phone calls. My friends roll their eyes
at me when we are out to coffee, and I keep jumping

for my phone. *We know*, they say. *You "have to take
this."* I apologize, excuse myself, check to see that

you are there. Nobody else notices how naked my
hands look. Nobody else thinks the space between

my chin and shoulder seems oddly empty. But I know
what this should feel like. I know what is missing.

At least the buzz of my cell phone fills the quiet.
For now, it will have to do. Until it can be replaced

by the sound of your padding feet and heavy breath,
by the sight of you in the doorway, exhausted and worn,

but finally, finally home.

The Shirt

The night I slept over, you lent me your shirt.
When I wore it out of the bathroom, you laughed
and said, *Oh, well. Now it's yours.*
I did not understand what you meant
but you insisted I keep it, so the first couple of nights
I wore it like a puddle, splashed through it,
trying to remember how the rain had felt.

When that failed, I found a photograph
of oranges and punched in the glass.
I stretched your shirt across the wood frame, made it a canvas.
I tried to paint swans, but I'm not a very good painter.
They look more like turtles on a bad hair day.
The next night I hung it on the flagpole and tried to signal the gods.
I don't think the gods read flags. That would make sense.
I made a hammock and tried to rest inside it,
but I may have stretched it out with all my wriggling.
I tossed it in the laundry with the other clothes
and the colors ran, it looks different than it did before.

The next time I saw you, I was embarrassed.
I had tried to make it into something beautiful,
I had done my best to find something new to show you.
You laughed again, your popcorn laugh,
and said, *You don't have to make it into anything.*
And I didn't understand, so you said,
Does it fit?
I said, *Yes.*

Then just wear it, silly.

Boom

This is what fireworks underwater feels like. Making out while eating Pop Rocks. Dynamite in a tin can, this is that time you left the popcorn in too long. There is a rodeo going on in your stomach, someone has started a pillow fight, and there are feathers everywhere. Eating cereal with no milk. Bumble bees in the dining room. Lightbulb wars. Someone is playing electric air guitar with the amp turned way up. Tongue on a battery. Socket sex. Lightning confetti. Ice cube Jawbreakers. Tinder lust.

Grace

I woke up this morning and said thank you.
To the ceiling, the bedsheets, the mirror, the windows.
To whomever was listening—

For the softly swaying hammock, the salt air,
the clouds that rolled in while I wasn't watching,
the sounds of someone starting a fire nearby,

the smell of a man's body, the sound of his sleepy baritone
from within the chest I pressed my head against—
the way his heart beat out of time with his quiet singing,

and his breath came out of time with both—
for the damp grass below us, and the swinging door
of the outdoor shower, for the goosebumps on his skin

from the darkling evening, for his patient arms around me
and the weight of him against me, and for the softly swaying
hammock, somehow large enough to carry all of this.

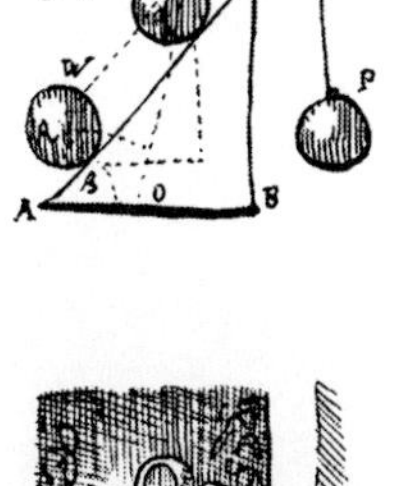

V.

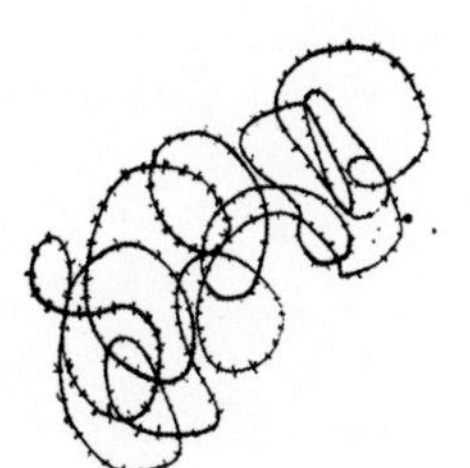

Until

For Franny

You love each other until the city becomes beautiful.
Until this gutter becomes a monument to that time you
needed menthols, in the pouring rain, in the summertime,
in the middle of the night. Until the street lamps lighting
the way to sundown become constellations guiding you home.

You love each other until you build yourself a city.
The couch is City Hall, the TV set is County Jail, the bed
is an elementary school playground. It is always recess.

You love each other until the city loves you back.
Lining up crosswalks with your doorstep, placing
taxicabs on corners. There is a deli with ice cream
up the block, you have everything you need.

You love the city, when you love each other.
And when you wake up in a city that you don't recognize,
and the traffic lights blink angry,

it is not because the city has grown cold.
It is not because your hands no longer fit in his.
It is because it is someone else's turn to lean
out her window into the cold cold morning and say,
Baby, look at all those traffic lights, blinking their way into dawn.

Scissors

When we moved in together,
I noticed—

You keep your scissors in the knife drawer.
I keep mine with the string and tape.

We both know how to hide our sharpest parts,
I just don't always recognize my own weaponry.

Something We Don't Talk About, Part II

how many times I said yes
how many times I said yes and yes and yes
because it was what you wanted to hear
and what I wanted you to hear
and what I wanted to want
and every time the walls
stayed above my head instead of
falling down upon me upon us
because if it was going to stop
then it would have to be me who said no
the walls were not going to help
and I didn't say no I didn't I never did
it was never your fault never yours
never mine only the walls that didn't tumble
when they should have
when they should have known
they should have been able to tell
when was the right time to fall

The Moves

You can tell she is counting exit signs.
You can tell she has left
her shoes by the door, laces already tied.

Leaving is an easy art to learn. But the
advanced steps—the pirouettes and arabesques
are difficult to master.

This is how I disappear in pieces.
This is how I leave while not moving from my seat.
This is how I dance away.
This is how I'm gone before you wake.

Postcards

I had already fallen in love with
far too many postage stamps,
when you appeared on my doorstep,
wearing nothing but a postcard promise.

No. *Appear* is the wrong word.
Is there a word for sucker-punching
someone in the heart?

Is there a word for when you are sitting
at the bottom of a roller coaster,
and you realize the climb is coming,
that you know what the climb means,
that you can already feel the flip in your
stomach from the fall, before you have
even moved—is there a word for that?
There should be.

You can only fit so many words in a postcard.
Only so many in a phone call.
Only so many into space, before you forget
that words are sometimes used for things
other than filling emptiness.

It is hard to build a body out of words.
I have tried. We have both tried.
Instead of laying your head on my chest,
I tell you about the boy who lives downstairs,
who stays up all night playing his drum set.
The neighbors have complained:
they have busy days tomorrow.
But he keeps on thumping through the night,
convinced, I think, that practice makes perfect.

Instead of holding my hand, you tell me about
the sandwich you made for lunch, the way the
pickles fit so perfectly against the lettuce.

Practice does not make perfect.
Practice makes permanent.
Repeat the same mistakes over and over,
and you don't get any closer to Carnegie Hall.
Even I know that.

Repeat the same mistakes over and over,
and you don't get any closer.
You—
never get any closer.

Is there a word for the moment you win
tug-of-war? When the weight gives,
and all that extra rope comes hurtling
towards you, how even though you've won,
you still end up with muddy knees and
burns on your hands?
Is there a word for that?
I wish there was.

I would have said it, when we were finally
alone together on your couch, neither one of us
with anything left to say.

Still now, I send letters into space,
hoping that some mailman somewhere
will track you down and recognize you
from the descriptions in my poems;

he will place the stack of them in your hands
and tell you, *There is a girl who still writes you.*
She doesn't know how not to.

Hiroshima

I.
When they bombed Hiroshima, the explosion formed a mini
supernova, so that every living animal, human, or plant that received
direct contact with the rays from that sun was instantly turned to ash.

What was left of the city soon followed.
The long-lasting damage from nuclear radiation
caused an entire city and its population to turn into powder.

II.
When I was born, my mom says I looked around the hospital room
with a stare that said, *This? I've done this before.*
She says that I have old eyes. When my Grandpa Genji died

I was only five years old, but I took my mom by the hand
and told her, *Don't worry, he'll come back as a baby.*
And yet, for someone who has apparently done this already,

I still haven't figured anything out yet.
My knees still buckle every time I get onstage.
My self-confidence can be measured out in teaspoons,

mixed into my poetry, and it still always tastes funny in my mouth.
But in Hiroshima, some people were wiped clean away leaving only
a wristwatch, a diary page, the mudflap from a bicycle.

So no matter that I have inhibitions to fill all my pockets,
I keep trying, hoping that one day I'll write the poem that I will be
proud to let sit in a museum exhibit as the only proof I existed.

III.
My parents named me Sarah, which is a biblical name.
In the original story, God told Sarah she could do something
impossible and she laughed. Because the first Sarah?

She didn't know what to do with Impossible.
And me? Well, neither do I. But I see the impossible every day.
Impossible is trying to connect in this world; trying to

hold on to others when things are blowing up around you; knowing
that while you are speaking, they aren't just waiting
for their turn to talk. They hear you.

They feel exactly what you feel at the same time that you feel it.
It's what I strive for every time I open my mouth:
That impossible connection.

IV.
There is a piece of wall in Hiroshima that was burnt black by the
radiation. But on the first step, a person blocked the rays from hitting
the stone. The only thing left is a permanent shadow of positive light.

After the A-Bomb, specialists said it would take seventy-five years for
the radiation-damaged soil of Hiroshima to grow anything again.
But that spring, there were new buds popping up from the earth.

When I meet you, in that moment,
I am no longer a part of your future.
I start quickly becoming part of your past.

But in that instant, I get to share a part of your present.
And you get to share a part of mine.
And that is the greatest present of all.

So if you tell me I can do the impossible, I will probably laugh at you.
I don't know if I can change the world. Yet.
Because I don't know that much about it.

And I don't know that much about reincarnation either,
but if you make me laugh hard enough,
sometimes I forget what century I'm in.

This isn't my first time here. This isn't my last time here.
These aren't the last words I'll share. But just in case,
I'm trying my hardest to get it right this time around.

VI.

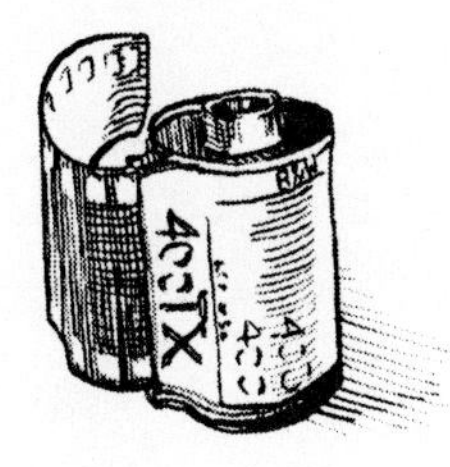

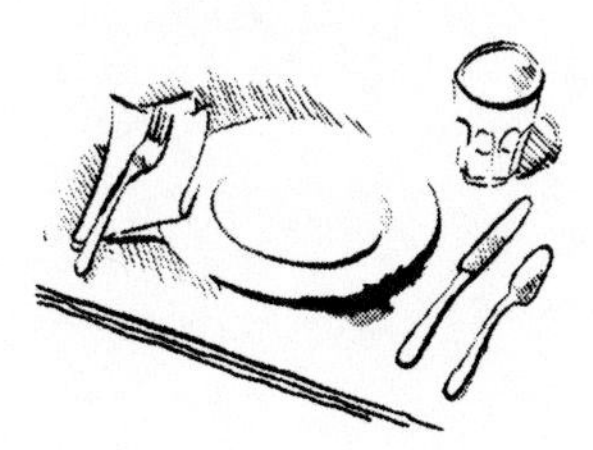

Extended Development

I.
It didn't always work this way.
There was a time you had to get your hands dirty,
when you were in the dark for most of it. Fumbling was a given.
When you needed more contrast, more saturation—
darker darks and brighter brights—they called it *extended development.*
It meant you spent longer time up to your wrists,
longer time inhaling chemicals. It wasn't always easy.

II.
Grandpa Stewart was a Navy photographer.
Young, red-faced, with his sleeves rolled up.
Fists of fingers like fat rolls of coins, in photographs he looked like
Popeye the Sailor Man come to life. Crooked smile, tuft of chest hair,
he showed up to World War II with a smirk and a hobby.
They asked him if he had much experience with photography,
and he lied. He learned to read Europe upside down
from the height of a fighter plane. Camera snapping, eyelids flapping,
the darkest darks and the brightest brights;
he learned war like it was a map, thought he could
read his way home. When other men returned,
they put their weapons out to rust, but he carried the lenses and the
cameras home with him. Opened a shop.
Turned it into a family affair.

III.
My father was born into a world of black and white.
His basketball hands learned the tiny clicks and slides
of lens into frame, film into camera, chemicals into plastic bins.
His father knew the equipment, but not the art;
he knew the darks, but not the brights.
My father learned the magic. Spent his time following light.
Once, he flew halfway across the country to follow a forest fire.
Hunted it with his camera. *Follow the light*, he said. *Follow the light.*

IV.
There are parts of me I only recognize from photographs.
The loft in Soho, on Wooster Street, with the creaky hallways and
twelve-foot ceilings, the white walls and cold floors.
This was my mother's home. Before she was *mother.*
Before she was *wife*. She was *artist.*
The only two rooms in the house with walls that reached up
to the ceilings and doors that could open and close were
the bathroom and the darkroom. The darkroom she made herself.
With custom-made stainless steel sinks
for washing prints, washing film.
An 8x10 bed enlarger that moved up and down by a giant
hand-crank. A bank of color-balanced lights, a white glass wall for
viewing prints, a hand-made drying rack that folded in and out
from the wall. My mother built herself a darkroom.
Made it her home. Fell in love with a man with basketball hands,
with the way he looked at light.

V.
They got married, had a baby, moved to a house near a park.
But they kept the loft on Wooster Street for birthday parties and
treasure hunts. The baby tipped the greyscale.
Filled her parents' photo albums with red balloons and yellow icing.
The baby grew into a girl without freckles. With a crooked smile.
She didn't understand why her friends did not have darkrooms
in their houses. She never saw her parents kiss
and she never saw them hold hands.
But one day another baby showed up—
this one with perfect straight hair and bubblegum cheeks,
and they named him Sweet Potato, and he laughed so loudly,
he scared the pigeons on the fire escape.
The four of them lived in the house near the park:
the Girl Without Freckles, the Sweet Potato Boy,
the Basketball Father, and Darkroom Mother,
and they lit their candles and said their prayers
and the corners of the photographs curled.

VI.
One day some towers fell.
And the house near the park became a house under ash,
so they escaped in backpacks, on bicycles, to darkrooms.
But the loft on Wooster Street was built for an artist,
not a family of pigeons. And walls that do not reach the ceiling
do not hold in the yelling. So the man with the basketball hands
put his weapons out to rust.
He could not go to war, and no maps pointed home.
His hands did not fit his wife's, did not fit the camera,
did not fit his body.
The Sweet Potato Boy mashed his fists into his mouth
until he had nothing more to say, and the Girl Without Freckles
went treasure-hunting on her own.

VII.
(And on Wooster Street, in Soho, in the building with the
creaky hallways, in the loft with the white walls, in the darkroom
with too many sinks, underneath the color-balanced lights,
she found a note tacked to the wall with a thumbtack,
left over from a time before towers. From a time before babies.
And the note said, *A guy sure loves a girl who works in the darkroom.)*

VIII.
It took a year for my father to pick up a camera again.
His first time out, he followed the Christmas lights
dotting their way through New York City's trees—
little flashes winking at him from out of the darkest darks.
A few years later, he flew across the country to follow a forest fire.
It was ravaging the west coast, eating eighteen-wheeler trucks
in its stride. He stayed for a week, hunting it with his camera.
On the other side of the country, I went to class and wrote a poem
in the margins of my notebook.
We have both learned the art of capture.
Maybe we are learning the art of embracing.
Maybe we are learning the art of letting go.

Questions and Answers, In No Particular Order

Never, not even once. Not even when I wished I could.

What color were the curtains? And the birds outside?

Olive oil. It was all we had. It made my skin soft, smelled for days.

Did you wear a helmet?

Autumn, mid-November. And any time I'm on a train.

How many rungs up the ladder before you knew?

Three-and-a-half times. Even though I lied about it at the time.

Did you regret it?

Blisters. And sore muscles. One skinned knee.

How many sugars with the tea?

L'horloge, minuit.

Where did you meet?

Tiny scraps of paper, mainly. But I kept them anyway.

Will this hurt?

Yes, every day of my life.

Loose Threads

The buttons on the sleeve of your jacket
were cracked in two. Both of them,

on your right arm, were missing their
other halves and existed in forlorn semicircles:

180 degrees of imperfection. Brown buttons
still clinging by a thread to your jacket material

despite their lack of wholeness, despite their
missing appendages. I wondered if you knew

that part of you was missing, I wondered
where the other halves had gone.

If they were together somewhere, lying on a dresser,
two halves that didn't fit together

because they belonged to two different buttons.
Or if you had lost them both independently:

one getting stuck on the turnstile at the subway,
the other falling off somewhere down a crowded hallway.

We ate sushi and talked about college
and work and basketball and didn't talk

about love and sex and loneliness
and friendship and buttons, half missing.

And I wondered if years from now,
you would remember where it was you lost me.

Private Parts

The first love of my life never saw me naked.
There was always a parent coming home in a half-hour,
always a little brother in the next room, always too much
body and not enough time for me to show him.

Instead, I gave him a shoulder, an elbow, the bend
of my knee. I lent him my corners, my edges:
the parts of me I could afford to offer, the parts of me
I had long since given up trying to hide.

He never asked for more. He gave me back his eyelashes,
the back of his neck, his palms. We held every piece we were given
like it was a nectarine—might bruise if we weren't careful—
we collected them like we were trying to build an orchard.

And the spaces that he never saw: the ones my parents
had labeled *private parts* when I was still small enough
to fit all of my self and worries inside a bathtub,
I made up for them by handing over all the private parts of me.

There was no secret I did not tell him,
there was no moment we did not share.
We didn't grow up, we grew in: like ivy wrapping,
molding each other into perfect yins and yangs.

We kissed with mouths open, breathing his exhale
into my inhale and back. We could have survived
underwater or in outer space, living only off the breath
we traded. We spelled *love* G-I-V-E.

I never wanted to hide my body from him.
If I could have, I am sure I would have given it all away
with the rest of me. I did not know it was possible
to keep some things for myself.

Some nights, I wake up knowing he is anxious.
He is across the world in another woman's arms and the years
have spread us like dandelion seeds, sanding down the edges of our
jigsaw parts that used to only fit each other.

He drinks from the pitcher on the nightstand, checks
the digital clock, it is five AM. He tosses in sheets and tries to settle.
I wait for him to sleep before tucking myself into elbows and knees,
reaching for things I have long since given away.

Another Missing

His absence is louder than a firework. I have misplaced all the silverware. Tonight I ate an entire meal of cauliflower. In lieu of doing laundry, I turned yesterday's shirt inside out. My windows don't close properly so the wind comes in uninvited. I guess you could say I miss him if missing him means that sometimes I forget to brush twice a day. I wear scarves now. Not because they're in fashion, but because it is cold in my room since the windows don't close. I wear socks too. I've been searching for words. I pee with the bathroom door open. I keep the light on, just in case.

The Call

You are at dinner with your beautiful fiancée.
She is wearing a light cotton dress and an
open cardigan (it is yours, she borrowed it
from your closet, you love it when she wears
your clothes, the way they smell like her for
days). The cardigan drapes off her
shoulders romantically. Her collarbone is
better than your high school poetry could
have imagined. Her hands are the size
of lily pads, she sets food upon the table.
Food she has cooked. For you. You are
going to marry this woman. She has
spent all day fighting the good fight.
She works daily for a better world to
raise your future children in. You love the
way she smells. The way she sets the
spoons upon the place mats. She sits
next to you, and unfolds her napkin.
You say grace and thank your gods for
each other. You taste the dinner. It
doesn't even taste vegetarian. She is
everything you could have hoped for. She
asks you about your day, rejoices in its tiny
victories. The boy you taught to understand
the mechanics of the pulley system, the
girl who finally stopped chatting in the corner.
You celebrate each other. And this is when
a phone call interrupts. It is me, wishing to
congratulate you on your engagement. I
apologize for catching you at dinner, you laugh
and tell me not to worry, you tell her I am on
the line. She smiles and says hello, I can hear
her in the background. You ask if I will be able
to attend the wedding, I tell you I wouldn't
miss it for the world. I wouldn't miss the
chance to see you so happy, to see you both

together in your new life. You say how glad
you are I've called, how we'll get together
soon, how you'll keep me posted on the registry,
the location of the rehearsal dinner. You hang
up and return to dinner, share a funny anecdote
about the two of us from college, she laughs
along and holds your hand; she says she can't
wait to meet me. After all the stories she's heard.

Or else.

When she picks up, I can hear the tightening
in the air as I tell her who I am. The fork scratching
across the dinner plate, the way she pretends
not to know the name, clears her throat
as she passes you the phone, says, *Honey,*
it's someone for you. But make it quick, will you?
No phone calls during dinner.

Flight

While I was taking out the trash tonight,
a toddler waddled past me, sticky-handed and
rash-cheeked, and I was left thinking
about the children you and I might have had.

It sounds silly now, with you so far on your
way to the future, and me so very here.

But I thought about his fingers gripping—
fists like small apricots—his grey eyes
as wet as puddles on concrete, his shaky
knees carrying him toward a crowd of pigeons,
waving his laughter into the sky.

I thought about wiping his nose on my sleeve,
(little boys are always snotting all over themselves)
I thought about the way his hand would reach.

And you, with your hat to block the sun,
your pants fitting exactly the way pants were made to fit,
a green t-shirt, a jacket that isn't warm enough.
I thought about you holding him around his waist,
his little-boy belly sliding beneath your hands,
the way you would lift him into the air, calling out to
the flock of pigeons that they forgot one, that they
left this little bird behind.

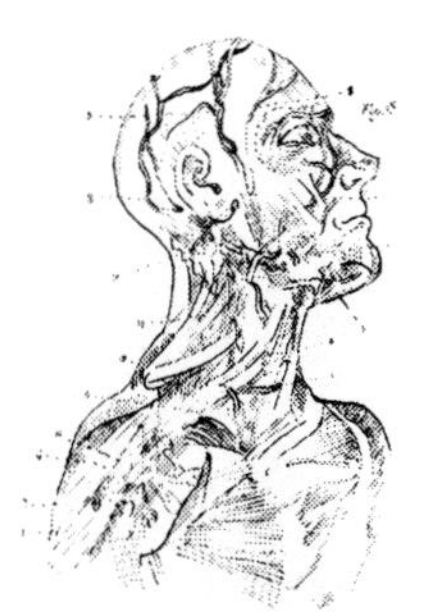

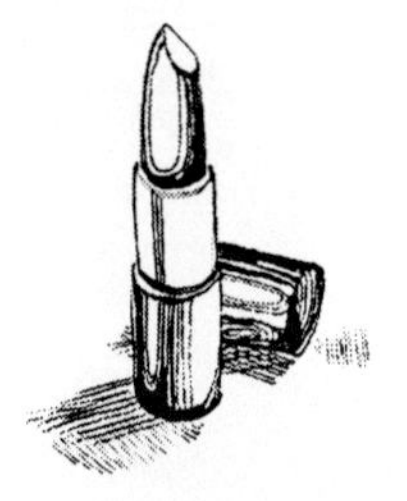

VII.

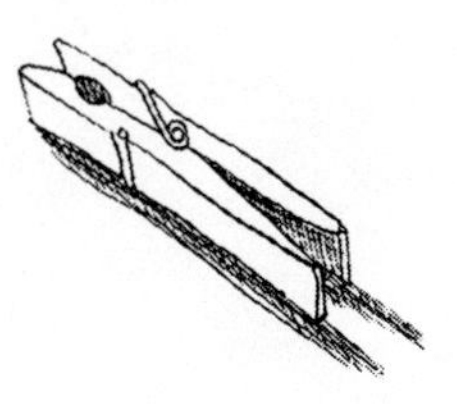

B

Instead of Mom, she's going to call me Point B.
Because that way she knows that no matter what happens,
at least she can always find her way to me.
And I'm going to paint the solar systems on the backs of her hands,

so she has to learn the entire universe before she can say,
Oh, I know that like the back of my hand.
And she's going to learn that this life will hit you hard, in the face,
wait for you to get back up, just so it can kick you in the stomach,

but getting the wind knocked out of you is the only way
to remind your lungs how much they like the taste of air.
There is hurt here that cannot be fixed by Band-Aids or poetry.
So the first time she realizes that Wonder Woman isn't coming,

I'll make sure she knows she doesn't have to wear the cape
all by herself. Because no matter how wide you stretch your fingers,
your hands will always be too small
to catch all the pain you want to heal. Believe me, I've tried.

And Baby, I'll tell her, don't keep your nose up in the air like that.
I know that trick; I've done it a million times.
You're just smelling for smoke
so you can follow the trail back to a burning house,

so you can find the boy who lost everything in the fire
to see if you can save him. Or else—
find the boy who lit the fire in the first place,
to see if you can change him.

But I know she will anyway.
So instead, I'll always keep
an extra supply of chocolate and rain boots nearby,
because there is no heartbreak that chocolate can't fix.

Okay, there's a few heartbreaks that chocolate can't fix.
But *that's* what the rain boots are for.
Because rain will wash away everything,
if you let it.

I want her to look at the world through the underside
of a glass-bottom boat, to look through a microscope at the galaxies
that exist on the pinpoint of a human mind,
because that's the way my mom taught me—

That there'll be days like this.
There'll be days like this, my mama said.
When you open your hands to catch,
and wind up with only blisters and bruises;

when you step out of the phone booth and try to fly, and
the very people you want to save are the ones standing on your cape;
when your boots will fill with rain,
and you'll be up to your knees in disappointment.

And *those* are the very days you have all the more reason
to say thank you. Because there's nothing more beautiful
than the way the ocean refuses to stop kissing the shoreline,
no matter how many times it's swept away.

You will put the wind in win(d)some, lose some.
You will put the star in starting over and over.
And no matter how many land mines erupt in a minute,
be sure your mind lands on the beauty of this funny place called life.

And yes, on a scale from one to over-trusting, I am pretty damn
naive. But I want her to know that this world is made out of sugar:
it can crumble so easily, but don't be afraid
to stick your tongue out and taste it.

Baby, I'll tell her, remember your mama is a worrier,
and your papa is a warrior, and you are the girl
with small hands and big eyes who never stops asking for more.
Remember that good things come in three's. And so do bad things.

And always apologize when you've done something wrong.
But don't you ever apologize for the way
your eyes refuse to stop shining;
your voice is small, but don't ever stop singing.

And when they finally hand you heartache,
when they slip war and hatred under your door,
and offer you handouts on street corners of cynicism and defeat,
you tell them that they *really* ought to meet your mother.

And Found

I am a god
of drawers left open.

It is easy to catch me in the act
of searching—
my keys
my self.

Careful.
Don't sit there.
You might knock over the pile of
confidence I took all day to stack.

I promise to tidy up before company arrives,
wouldn't want my socks and daydreams all over the carpet.

Sure, I know where most things are but
give me enough time and I can lose anything.

I have had enough practice
at sliding things under the bed when no one is watching.

And I know
you are always in the last place I look.

Winter Without You

Tonight, Brooklyn was so cold,
it pulled itself a little closer to Manhattan
just to have something warm to lie next to.

Earlier this week, I stacked a pile of laundry
fresh from the drier and dove in it like it was
autumn leaves, like I thought I could stop the fading,
could keep the colors if I held them in my hands.

Winter has arrived like the stray cat
who patrols my neighborhood—
annoyed by my foolish surprise
at its sudden appearance.

My building's Super rang my doorbell
this afternoon and came in to change
the knob on my heater. I greeted him
in flannel pajama pants and a sweatshirt.

Oh, thank goodness, I laughed. The heat
has been clanking all night, and it keeps
me awake. He considered the pile of
unfolded laundry and 1 PM pajamas.
Just you? He asked. Just me.

It is December, and nobody asked if I was ready.

Corey's Turn

In retrospect
squeezing my knees shut
does not seem like the most effective move
and certainly not the bravest
but at the time
it was as fast as I could think
I knew that Corey
was tall and strong but that
was not the concern at the moment
because he had stayed on his side
of the table facing me
watching my face
whereas Mark was the one
whose turn it was to be dared
in truth
I think it might have even been
his idea
or both of them together
laughing as they whispered
the word between them
loud enough for anyone in
third-grade art class to hear
except the teacher who was busy
at someone else's watercolor station
so it was Mark who was supposed
to kiss me
there
below the table
Mark whose red hair curled as perfect
as a children's rhyme on his
freckled forehead
Mark
the shortest boy in class
who would have been teased for it
if he wasn't so funny
Mark who made me laugh in math

whose breath I could now feel
on my shins
and I don't remember if I wore a skirt
or pants
but I do know that Corey watched
me the entire time
even as I continued to watercolor
pretending that I did not see Mark
on his hands and knees below me
instead of calling for the teacher
instead of tattletaleing
instead of kicking him in the jaw
I held my knees together
and eventually he gave up waiting
kissed my knees instead and
emerged from below the table
claiming that technically he had completed
the dare since that was as close
as he could get
that surely that should still count
surely it was now Corey's Turn.

Witness

I do not ignore bubble letters on the bathroom stall.
The pretty cursive, the delicate loop in the y.

When the words spell, *help me. I hate my life*,
I am here to witness your toilet paper autobiography.

No judgment. I have spent hours wondering
how many other people's photographs I have wandered into.

Who takes the time to notice I was here?
What remains to be seen?

That couple from Minnesota in Times Square at Christmas.
The bottom left-hand corner.

There I am wearing my blue coat.
Trying to turn away from the camera, blurry.

Yolk

For the guy who threw an egg at me from his car window.

Hey. Thanks for coming. You know, I haven't ever done one of these before, and I didn't know whether you'd show up, so I'm glad I recognized you.

I mean, you were exactly like your description said you'd be—
Big black sports car,
muscular ego,
really good aim.

And I'm glad, because I hate when people advertise themselves as something they're not, and then you meet them in person and are disappointed. It's why I don't wear makeup. So you always know that what you see is pretty much what you get.

That's why *my* description reads:
Skin—inclined towards bruising.
Hair for days—of face hiding.
Big, giant—self-consciousness that you can really just
grab with both hands.

I'm glad we're both honest.

Look, I know it's past my bedtime and a nice girl like me probably shouldn't be out on the street, but if you get to know me better, you'll find my eyelashes are the most stubborn part of me.

They love late night haunts, wouldn't trade them for all the pillows in the world. Plus, if I were at home right now, this street corner never would have served its purpose: the perfect spot for this rendezvous.

You—tall, dark, and speeding.
Me—bottomless pit of bad reflexes.
What a perfect match.

I wish I'd had more time to prepare, could have gotten more dressed up for the occasion. Now I'm embarrassed, really. That you put in so much effort, and here I am wearing nothing but an easy target.

Accidents

One time, there was an X-ray accident.
It left me with a transparent chest.

Sometimes this is inconvenient: like during job interviews
or first kisses. Sometimes it's not so bad.

Like when the hummingbird orchestra is in town
and they need a substitute conductor.

Once there was a laundry accident.
Now everything I own looks like a Funfetti cake.

Once there was a microwave accident.
It melted my shoulders into old crayon tops.

Now I have stopped counting the accidents.
So they don't count as accidents.

Now they are just decisions.
Like the mousetrap decision,

which scared me awake again.
Or the refrigerator decision, which left me

with melting ice cream and a chilly apartment.
Or the locked bathroom door decision,

which left me with an . . . accident. Listen.
There is a hummingbird inside my chest.

He is cranky with me. He has been waiting
to go to sleep for hours, and I have kept him

awake with my racket. Once there was a ceiling fan accident.
Now there is broken glass everywhere and I can't turn off the lights.

Once there was a boyfriend accident. I mean decision.
An iceberg accident, a poison apple accident.

Sometimes I invite experts to help figure out what is going wrong.
They take a look inside and check the wiring,

they tell me someone has placed the panic button
awfully close to the ignition. There has been a motorcycle accident,

now nobody can stop staring. There was a domino accident,
and my days fall into each other faster than I can catch them.

There is a beach in Montauk where the rocks are piled
from the shoreline to the dunes. When the water pulls in

across the stones they knock together like broken bones
and you can feel the ground below you shift and move.

But when the sea rolls out, each pebble
knocks and tumbles down the shore.

The accidental orchestra plays between the rocks—
like loud applause—the ocean cries, Encore!

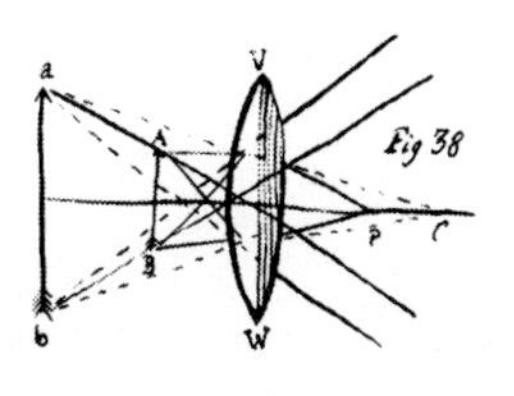

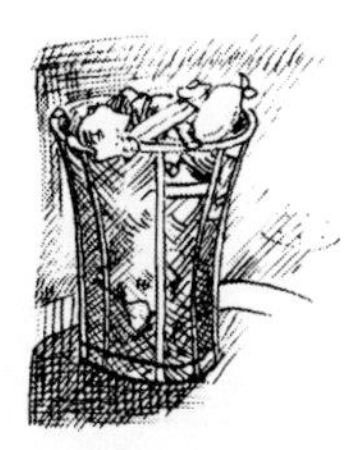

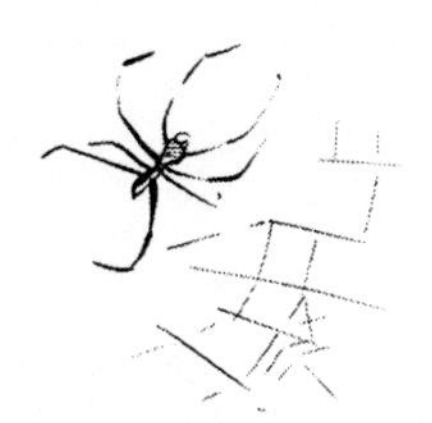

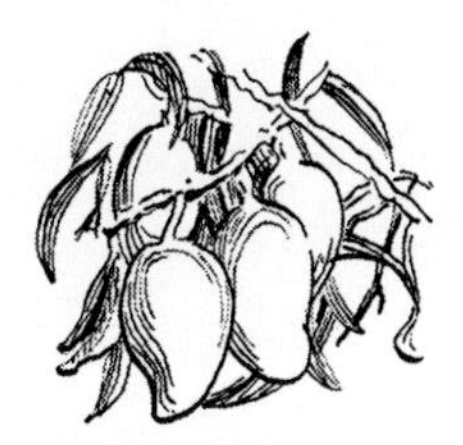

VIII.

Peacocks

Lately? Lately I've been living with spiders.
But as roommates go, they haven't been too bad.
The one in the bathroom keeps to his side of the tile,
and the one in the bedroom can get a little bit grabby,
but for the most part he keeps his hands to himself.

I guess all those car engines and hairsprays finally caught up to us
because the sky here is so polluted, it glows orange
from 5PM, through night, 'til morning.
Some people think it's disgusting
that you can shower off what you thought was a tan.
But me? I can't help but fall in love with a city
that has fifteen hours of twilight.

Outside the city, the dark is so dark,
it is easy to forget which day is Tuesday.
But the night there was a dry lightning storm,
it was like strobe lights through the window.
I snuck outside and stood with my face up, smiling:
I thought God was taking photographs.
And even though I felt silly standing there in my underwear,
I figured I needn't be embarrassed: he's seen me in a whole lot less.

Some nights, I wake up with a black hole in my chest.
It echoes like a beatboxing hurricane
and burns like a grandmother's memory.
I tried Pepcid AC. It didn't help.

I gave a haircut with big sloppy scissors
and even made it look sort of nice.
Everybody knew it was just a courtesy cut anyway;
it probably wouldn't do anything for the lice or the bedbugs.

I've been looking for my favorite constellations everywhere,
but I haven't found any sign of them yet.

The distances between stars are all different here. Much wider.
I have always relied on the English of others and in this
Rickshaw Named Desire, it's no exception.

On a cement rooftop somewhere off the highway,
it is creeping its way towards night, when nineteen-year-old Ravi
begs me to write a love letter for him.
It is for Neha, the girl he is in love with.
She speaks English. He does not.
So he cannot explain to me that this is forbidden.
That he is already set to marry—whomever his parents choose.
But certainly someone within the village,
and certainly someone within the caste,
and certainly not this someone, wrapped in yellow silk,
who smiles up at me from the photograph he shows me.

I write it for him anyway.
It has something about *the moon*, some *stars in the sky*,
the way her *eyes sparkle* and how *he wishes they could be together always.*

When I finish writing, Ravi takes the letter from my hands
and reads it carefully out loud. He does not understand a single word,
but reads diligently and slowly, looking up at me every so often
to see if he is pronouncing the words correctly.
When I hear what I have written out loud,
the clichés hang in the air between us like bad breath.
I wish that I could take it back and write it over.

I would write:

> Dear Neha,
> Be careful about rooftops. Not about how high they are, but about how quickly your heart beats the faster you climb. Ravi's hands are good for climbing. I like the way he stands behind his mother when she is working: not so much to insist on helping her, but just to let her feel his presence, in case she needs him to reach for something on a top shelf. I like that he believes in love letters. His pants are a few inches too short. Have you come to visit him here? Probably not. The peacocks

are enormous. They sound like cats. No one seems to pay them very much mind, but the males dance across all the rooftops of the village, begging for someone to notice their tails.

Good luck with your secret,
Sarah

Ravi gets to the end of his letter, and reads the words, *I love you*. These are words he understands. He smiles an enormous smile and bows his head. On my way back to the car, the translator tells me Ravi wishes to say thank you. I tell him to tell Ravi good luck, and he does so. Ravi puts both hands inside the car window onto my own and says, *Dhanyavad*—over and over, thanking me for the love letter—*bahut bahut dhanyavad.*

He will never marry her, the translator tells me,
after we have been driving in the dark for a few minutes.
Yes, I say, *but he can love her.*

It is monsoon season.
I watch as tall street corners become river banks and
potholes become death traps; not even the rickshaws are safe.
The cobra that I met in the orchard behind the lantern shed
was much smaller than I'd imagined,
but the mangoes were just as sweet.
That's probably why when we cut one open,
a spider crawled its way out. It had made its home inside.

On Being Prepared

I. Now.
Sometimes, when I am by myself,
I imagine my own murder.
The open window,
the three steps necessary to cross the room.
Blunt object to the skull,
red ribbon and the feel of the carpet against my cheek.
I fix my hair in the mirror,
change the song to one with cello.
When they find me,
someone will check the time of death.
Someone will do the math, count backwards
through the music.
Press the buttons, back, back, back.
They will figure out which song was playing
when it happened.
Even when nobody is home,
I am careful what I listen to.

II. Then.
I used to practice
what I would look like
when someone was falling in love with me.
I tilted my head, looked into the distance.
I don't even notice you falling in love with me, I practiced to the mirror.
I am too preoccupied with what I am doing.
Nobody wants to be noticed when they are falling in love.
It is a private moment.
Whoever was falling in love with me, I reasoned,
deserved not to be disturbed.

III. Sometime.
I am working in my pajamas.
There is a knock at the door.
Teeth unbrushed, hair unwashed.
I leave everything to answer.
You kiss me and take off your coat.

Don't have long to spare, you say.
Just came by to say hello.
In the other room, my music skips.
The carpet squishes between my toes.
I wasn't expecting you.

On the Discomfort of Being in the Same Room as the Boy You Like

Everyone is looking at you looking at him.
Everyone can tell. *He can tell.* So you
spend most of your time not looking at him.
The wallpaper, the floor, there are cracks
in the ceiling. Someone has left a can of
iced tea in the corner, it is half-empty,
I mean half-full. There are four light bulbs
in the standing lamp, there is a fan. You
are counting things to keep from looking
at him. Five chairs, two laptops, someone's
umbrella, a hat. People are talking so you
look at their faces. This is a good trick. They
will think you are listening to them and not
thinking about him. Now he is talking. So
you look away. The cracks in the ceiling are
in the shape of a whale or maybe an elephant
with a fat trunk. If he ever falls in love with
you, you will lie on your backs in a field
somewhere and look up at the sky and he will
say, *Baby, look at that silly cloud, it is a whale!*
and you will say, *Baby, that is an elephant*
with a fat trunk, and you will argue for a bit,
but he will love you anyway.

He is asking a question now and no one has
answered it yet. So you lower your eyes from
the plaster and say, *The twenty-first, I think,*
and he smiles and says, *Oh, cool*, and you
smile back, and you cannot stop your smiling,
oh, you cannot stop your smile.

Here and Now

Here and now, I have only these hands,
this mouth, this skin as wide as a shoreline,
this beehive between my ears, this buzz, this buzz.
You are the best thing I never planned.
This is the widest I can stretch my arms without
dropping things. This is the first time I don't care
if I drop things. This is what dropping
things feels like. This is what happens when
the flowers wake up one morning and decide to
smell human: it confuses us, makes us
reach backwards into places that are sharp,
feel around for things we've dropped. I have
forgotten what I was looking for. It doesn't
seem important. You brought me flowers.
You made the bed. This is the widest I can
stretch my arms. This is all I have right now.

Open

Sometimes, when we kiss, I keep my eyes open. I know it's impolite. It started when I was in high school, the first boy—the one who tasted like peach vitamin water and sweat—he kissed me as though I was made of tears and he had never seen the sea before. I was scared he would look at me, scared that if he opened his eyes, I would turn into a pillar of salt, so I peeked to make sure he didn't. First one eye and then the other, our mouths a tightrope, my eyes a set of cheeky clowns trying not to fall. I had never seen another person so up-close before. Things happen to God's perfect aesthetic. Noses are mountain slopes, cheeks are fields, lips gape and pull, morph and stretch, we are no longer faces, we are landscapes. I was not kissing a boy, I was kissing America. And America tasted like peach vitamin water and sweat.

Now it is a habit. Now, it is less about fear and more about curiosity. Today I opened my eyes, and this man—the one who makes the bed when I leave—his eyes were open too. I was embarrassed, and I was furious! Nobody opens their eyes when they kiss! How dare he look at me when I did not know! But when I pulled away from him, he was smiling; he had not blinked. He does not kiss me like an ocean. His eyes do not turn me to salt. This is new terrain.

A Place to Put Our Hands

My wheels are finally
slowing down.

You are trying to find
a place to put your hands.
I am trying to find
a way back to India.

Maybe we are both looking
for the same soil:
it is red, smells like clay,
the way it must have smelled
when God put it there.

I am not scared
the way I was once.
I have bled through
the train to Agra,
fought the cockroaches
with my bare hands.
I have seen the Taj Mahal
at sunrise, I remember
what love and pain can build.

You are looking
for mountains to climb.
I am looking
for the words to a poem
I can't remember.

Today's Poem

Sometimes the writing
should be put on hold: a boy
who smells like springtime.

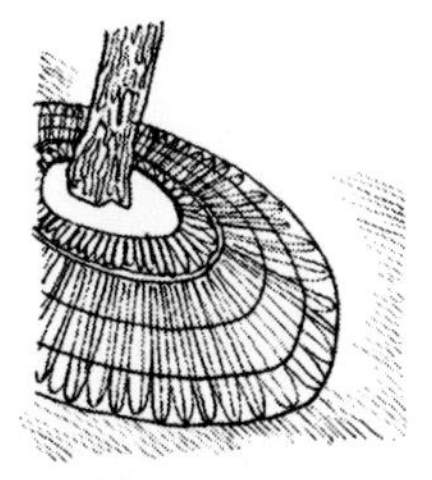

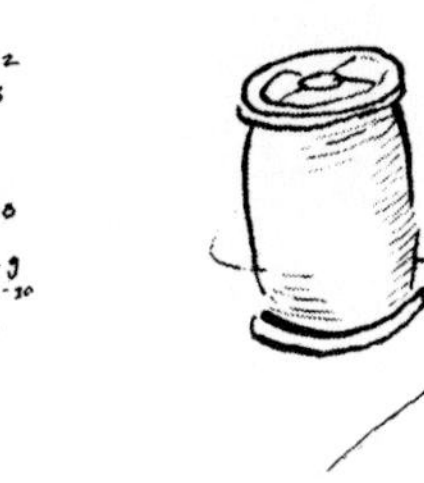

IX.

Ghost Ship

In the second grade, every song was a handful of orange Tic Tacs
rolling around my tongue: I knew all the words, could feel them
tangy, round, and smooth, but didn't care which one was which.
I could sing back the Beatles perfectly with the words
all smashed together. I was the first one to memorize
any song the music teacher sang us. My favorite was *The Ghost Ship*.
The words meant nothing to me, but the melody was full
of ragged sails and midnight hurricanes. It was all port and starboard,
I sang it 'til the winds ran out of me.

My little brother was four years younger, but two steps ahead.
He memorized the shapes my mouth made, practiced them tirelessly.
We shoved the words at each other as though it was a competition
to see who could get them out the fastest, who could
draw them out the longest. *And the cold wind blew.*
By the time it was his turn to learn it in music class four years later,
he already knew the song so well, he confused the teacher.
My fist-chested brother. A fireplace shotgun, waiting for his chance.

⋆

Little girls learn how to sing *The Perfect Man*
before we ever know what the lyrics mean.
Strong arms, good hair, wide eyes, brave heart, big money, kind hands.
We build model ships in bottles,
whispering life into the toothpicks and wire;
we make plans and blueprints for the one we hope is coming.
And come they do. Fleets of vessels. Battleships and barges.
They arrive on the horizon, flags to the sky.

I have seen what can happen when a woman tries to make a dinghy
into a galleon. Sometimes a rowboat is all you need.
Sometimes a whaler. A ferry.
Our model ships look perfect in their bottles,
but we do not know if they are seaworthy.
Sometimes the one that reaches your harbor
has already been through the storm.

Sometimes you cannot see the leaking until you are so close.
Until you are already out to sea.
Trying to batten down the hatches.
Bailing the water pooling at your ankles.
Manning the rigging alone.

My little brother pushed off from shore before the tide
had turned his way. Always two steps ahead.
For years, I didn't want him going under.
I tried to anchor him against the storms,
threw him safety nets and buoys, trained myself in CPR.
I have known so many men whose hulls have been made hollow
by the salt of this sea, whose sails are pulled so tightly into the wind,
whose rudders no longer point to anything but drowning.
How do you keep a boy floating?
How do you keep him above the ache?

Men will drift eternal. Men will say, *It's just a scratch*,
when the cannons have shot them full of holes.
They will look at their tiny driftwood tied with strings and say, *Ship*.
They will look at the broken wheel between their hands
and say, *Captain*. They will look to the men
who have jumped overboard without them and say, *Crew*.

Today my brother is twenty-years handsome. He is smirk and motor.
Femur strong and decision heavy. His decks have been worn down
by the feet of others, but his compass always points north.
I can hear the cabin creak. The chains rattle. The ladders sag.
It has been a decade since I heard him sing.

*

We are in Ireland, a country to which we have never been.
I have rented us a car I cannot drive and have been gracelessly
maneuvering us through the green, green countryside
toward the cliffs of the western coast.
The rain is a diligent mother who checks on us every few hours.
The sky is endless grey. My brother's quiet fills the car
like a family holiday. I turn on the radio to mask the fog.
The coast arrives beneath us suddenly, the way all shorelines do:

full and vast, crumbling away at all our stubborn solidness.
And there, standing against the crashing sea,
sits the massive body of a shipwreck,
as though all of history has been gifted to us.

We are giddy with adventure. We are skipping over the rocks,
shouting to the wild horses and the ocean's roar.
The jagged porthole opens to us, we pull ourselves
into the boat's hungry mouth. It is empty and whole.
Full speed ahead. Prow to stern. Fore and aft.
We climb until we are scraped and muddy.
Rust children with lighthouse eyes.

And together we start to sing the words we have known since
childhood. As though they have been drifting through us, lost at sea,
waiting for the right current to find safe harbor.

Oh, Brother. No matter your wreckage.
There will be someone to find you beautiful,
despite the cruddy metal. Your ruin is not to be hidden
behind paint and canvas. Let them see the cracks.
Someone will come to sing into these empty spaces.
Their voice will echo off your insides like a second-grader
and her little brother—four years younger, two steps ahead.
Singing 'til the metal vibrates. 'Til the ghost ship rings.

(During his marriage to the poet Sylvia Plath, Ted Hughes took up an affair with Assia Wevill around 1962. Wevill's husband, David, upon finding out about the affair, took a number of sleeping pills and attempted suicide, but survived. After Plath's suicide in 1963, Wevill moved into Hughes's house two days after Plath's death. Of Hughes, Wevill told friends that his lovemaking was so ferocious, "in bed, he smells like a butcher." She helped raise Plath and Hughes's children, and one of her own, but Hughes once again left on another affair in 1968. The following year, Wevill committed suicide and the murder of her four-year-old daughter, gassing herself in the same manner that Plath had done. In her diary, Assia Wevill wrote that the ghost of Plath had made her suicidal.)

Lightning

To Assia Wevill

Were there nights
when you were sure he would grind you down to bone?
That you had not placed nearly enough wax paper on the bedspread,
that you would have to wash the sheets tomorrow?

Did you ever think of David?
His custard eyes
and balloon hands.
Clumsy with words
and careless with love.

Some of us are born chasing disaster.
From the moment we enter this world screaming,
we are looking for lightning,
the raw of our bodies
always searching for cleaver hands.

You memorized every love poem he wrote for someone else
and slept on a pillow that had held her slumber.

Some of us are born chasing poetry.
When you searched for the words,
was it her voice who spoke them?

The Type

Everyone needs a place. It shouldn't be inside of someone else. —Richard Siken

If you grow up the type of woman men want to look at,
you can let them look at you.

Do not mistake eyes for hands.
Or windows. Or mirrors.

Let them see what a woman looks like.
They may not have ever seen one before.

If you grow up the type of woman men want to touch,
you can let them touch you.

Sometimes it is not you they are reaching for.
Sometimes it is a bottle. A door. A sandwich.

A Pulitzer. Another woman.
But their hands found you first.

Do not mistake yourself for a guardian.
Or a muse. Or a promise. Or a victim. Or a snack.

You are a woman. Skin and bones. Veins and nerves. Hair and sweat.
You are not made of metaphors. Not apologies. Not excuses.

If you grow up the type of woman men want to hold,
you can let them hold you.

All day they practice keeping their bodies upright—
even after all this evolving, it still feels unnatural,

still pulls tight the muscles, strains the arms and spine.
Only some men want to learn what it feels like to wrap themselves

into a question mark around you, admit they do not have the answers
they thought they would have by now;

some men will want to hold you like The Answer.
You are not the answer.

You are not the problem. You are not the poem
or the punchline or the riddle or the joke.

Woman. If you grow up the type men want to love,
you can let them love you.

Being loved is not the same thing as loving.
When you fall in love, it is discovering the ocean

after years of puddle jumping. It is realizing you have hands.
It is reaching for the tightrope when the crowds have all gone home.

Do not spend time wondering if you are the type of woman
men will hurt. If he leaves you with a car-alarm heart,

you may learn to sing along. It is hard to stop loving the ocean.
Even after it has left you gasping, salty.

Forgive yourself for the decisions you have made,
the ones you still call mistakes when you tuck them in at night.

And know this.

Know you are the type of woman
who is looking for a place to call yours.

Let the statues crumble.
You have always been the place.

You are a woman who can build it yourself.
You were born to build.

Astronaut

I see the moon and the moon sees me.
The moon sees somebody that I don't see.
God bless the moon and God bless me.
God bless the somebody that I don't see.
If I get to heaven before you do,
I'll make a hole and pull you through.
I'll write your name on every star.
And that way the world won't seem so far.
—*Children's rhyme*

The astronaut will not be at work today. He has called in sick. He has turned off his cell phone, his laptop, his pager, his alarm clock. There is a fat yellow cat asleep on his couch, rain against the windows, and not even the hint of coffee in the kitchen air.

Everyone is in a tizzy. The engineers on the fifteenth floor have stopped working on their particle machine, the anti-gravity room is leaking, and even the freckled kid with glasses (whose only job is to clean out the trash) is nervous: fumbles the bag, spills a banana peel

and a paper cup. Nobody notices. They are too busy recalculating what this will mean for lost time.
How many galaxies are we losing per minute;
how long before the next rocket can be launched?

Somewhere—An electron flies off its energy cloud.
A black hole has erupted.
A mother has finished setting the table for dinner.
A *Law & Order* marathon is starting.

The astronaut is asleep.
He has forgotten to turn off his watch,
which ticks against his wrist like a metal pulse.
He does not hear it. He dreams of coral reefs and plankton.

His fingers find the pillowcase's sailing masts.
He turns on his side, opens his eyes once.
He thinks that scuba divers must have
the most wonderful job in the world.
So much water to glide through.

The Paradox

When I am inside writing,
all I can think about is how I should be outside living.

When I am outside living,
all I can do is notice all there is to write about.

When I read about love, I think I should be out loving.
When I love, I think I need to read more.

I am stumbling in pursuit of grace,
I hunt patience with a vengeance.

On the mornings when my brother's tired muscles
held to the pillow, my father used to tell him,

For every moment you aren't playing basketball,
someone else is on the court practicing.

I spend most of my time wondering
if I should be somewhere else.

So I have learned to shape the words *thank you*
with my first breath each morning, my last breath every night.

When the last breath comes, at least I will know I was thankful
for all the places I was so sure I was not supposed to be.

All those places I made it to,
all the loves I held, all the words I wrote.

And even if it is just for one moment,
I will be exactly where I am supposed to be.

In the Event of an Emergency

Return my teeth to the baseball bat.
Return my right leg to the car bumper.
Return my right hand to the first boy who held it,
Return my left hand to my father.

You can find the jewelry in the chimney,
buried under photographs of my grandfather.
Return his smile to him.
Wash my mouth out first. Thoroughly.
Return it to my mother. It has always been hers.
Return the poetry to my first-grade teacher.
Apologize for the time I went snooping through her desk.
Return the journals to the traveling salesman,
I bought everything he sold.
If there is any music left, you can untie it from my throat.
It was dying there anyway.

All the loose skin, return it to the sun.
Return the pads of my feet to the tree in the front yard.
Let the one who loves me make a pillow of my hair.
Give my left ear to my brother,
I was always waiting for him to take it.
Give my right ear to the thunder,
I should have given it long ago.

And in case there is an empty stomach, in case an empty womb—
give these to the women made of ambulances.
Give it to the sirens' scream, the flashing lights.
Let them use the hunger as an engine,
let them use the womb to nurse a tiny tulip to this earth.
Let it be a home for a mouse to crawl inside of.
Let winter not find its way here.
Return this last place to the swift birds,
let them finally find a place to pause,
a nest in which to keep each other warm.

Notes

Love Poem #137 "too many commas" is a phrase from playwright Will Eno. In fact, a few chunks of this poem were inspired by him. The original context is a monologue from his play "Thom Pain" which goes, "He did not love too much, nor too well, but with too much sweat, shit, and fear, with too many long words, too many commas."

Subway Disclaimer: I have no idea if this actually works. I do know that at the subway station at 96th and Broadway, you can look up and see the street above you. I always wondered if this would be dangerous in the rain. Maybe they have some sort of mechanism that catches the rain before it slips down to the trains. But maybe not. This poem was written in November 2004.

The Oak Tree Speaks The original ad for Manhattan Mini Storage reads: "Raising a baby in an NYC apartment is like growing an oak tree in a thimble."

The Toothbrush to the Bicycle Tire This poem was written in November 2009.

Montauk The line, "There are places where fishnets do not mean stockings," is actually from an old real estate ad for Keeshan Real Estate. I think the original ad said, "Montauk: Where fishnets aren't stockings." I believe this poem was written in September 2010.

Brother I believe this poem was written sometime in the spring of 2009.

Hands This is the original version of this poem. The version that most folks are familiar with is the one that aired on *Russell Simmons Presents Def Poetry Jam* on HBO, but that was edited for time. The first version of this poem was created in December 2004.

Jellyfish This poem was written and first performed in 2006.

The Ladder This poem was first shared in an interview with Cristin O'Keefe Aptowicz for her "Live from the Amy Clampitt House" series on the *IndieFeed Performance Poetry* podcast in August 2013.

BRICKLAYER This poem was written in April 2009.

FOREST FIRES This poem was written in September 2009.

HAND-ME-DOWNS This poem was first performed in November 2007 at SkinText:Brown University's WORD! poetry show.

SHOSHOLOZA I wrote this poem after visiting the District Six Museum in Cape Town, South Africa. I learned about the story of Noor Ebrahim and his pigeons from a photograph in the museum, and I added details. Every proper noun I use in this poem is taken directly from information and exhibits in the museum (the names of streets, stores, etc.) The way I've spelled the lyrics is merely a rough transliteration. This poem was originally written in December 2006 and was first performed at the Bowery Poetry Club for Beau Sia's Incantations Show in January 2007.

INDIA TRIO This poem was written in July 2010 during my second trip to India. I was working on two documentary projects via an AT&T New Media Fellowship through the Watson Institute for International Studies at Brown University. I was living with Maggie Sarin and her family and was also hosted by Arati Kaul and the Pragati School.

PAWS This poem is inspired by Cristin O'Keefe Aptowicz's poem "Hound."

SCISSORS This poem was inspired by a Facebook status posted by my friend, rapper Black Cracker.

HIROSHIMA This poem was written after a trip to Japan with my cousins in June 2006. The objects that I mention ("a wristwatch, a diary page, the mudflap from a bicycle") are all actual objects on display at the Hiroshima Peace Memorial Exhibit. I performed this poem on the semi-final stage at the National Poetry Slam in Austin, Texas in August 2006, thanks to my generous teammates on the NYC Urbana Poetry Slam team: Jeanann Verlee, Jamie Kilstein, and Akua Doku. (Plus our coach Shappy Seasholtz.)

Extended Development This poem was originally written for the Providence, RI chapter of *The Encyclopedia Show*, "Volume 3: The Visual Spectrum of Color." The original Encyclopedia Show format was founded in Chicago by Robbie Q. Telfer and Shanny Jean Maney. For the show I participated in, I was given my assignment by Megan Thoma to write a poem about "Colorfulness, Chroma, Saturation." This poem was first performed in November 2010.

Questions and Answers, In No Particular Order I found a list of writing prompts from *The Journal Newsletter* by Susan Michael and David Michael that included the prompt, "write a series of questions and answers to compose a poem."

Loose Threads This poem was originally written in December 2005.

Private Parts This poem was written and first performed in April 2009.

B This poem was first written in May 2007. It was performed quite a few times, but is most well known for the performance I gave as the opening of my TEDTalk in February 2011. It was then published as a hardcover book by The Domino Project and illustrated by Sophia Janowitz in November 2011. The line, "There'll be days like this, my mama said," is from the song "Mama Said" by Luther Dixon and Willie Denson, made famous by The Shirelles in 1961.

Corey's Turn This poem was written during my time as the Serenbe Artist in Residency in October 2013.

And Found This poem was originally written in May 2007.

Peacocks I wrote this poem after I returned from my first trip to India in 2008. The trip was thanks to Brown University's chapter of the Students of the World organization and the Lighting a Billion Lives campaign run by The Energy and Resources Institute in New Delhi.

On the Discomfort of Being in the Same Room as the Boy You Like This poem was written in April 2009.

Ghost Ship The song I refer to is "The Ghost Ship" from Don Besig and Nancy Price's "Reflections of a Lad at Sea." That is also where the line, "And the cold wind blew," is from. The shipwreck cited in this poem is the "Plassy," located on Inis Oírr of the Aran Islands.

Lightning This poem was written in April 2009. The introductory paragraph is based on information from *A Lover of Unreason: The Life and Tragic Death of Assia Wevill* by Yehuda Koren and Eilat Negev.

The Type The line, "Everyone needs a place. It shouldn't be inside of someone else," is from Richard Siken's poem "Detail of the Woods." This poem was first performed in Jacqueline Novogratz's living room and later thoroughly workshopped by the women of the Pink Door Poetry Summit hosted by Rachel McKibbens.

Astronaut This poem was first written in April 2009. When I perform this poem, I begin by singing the nursery rhyme. The words are from my childhood, but the melody is one I made up.

The Paradox The earliest form of this poem was written in April 2009.

In the Event of an Emergency This poem was also prompted by Susan Michael and David Michael's list of writing prompts.

Several illustrations in this book are drawn after images from the 1851 edition of *The Iconographic Encyclopedia of Science, Literature and Art* as reprinted in *The Complete Encyclopedia of Illustration* by J. G. Heck (1979).

Credits

Thanks to the following publications and journals, in which some of these poems first appeared in slightly different forms:

The Bakery, "Private Parts"

Damselfly Press, "Witness"

decomP, "Lightning"

Foundling Review, "New York, June 2009"

The Huffington Post, "The Type"

Jewels of Elul, "Poppy"

La.Lit Magazine, "Jellyfish," "Paws," "Forest Fires," "Winter Without You"

The Legendary, "Hands," "The Discomfort of Being in the Same Room as the Boy You Like," "Slivers," "Montauk"

Literary Bohemian, "Peacocks" (excerpt)

Pear Noir!, "India Trio"

Thrush Poetry Journal, "The Oak Tree Speaks"

Treehouse Magazine, "Yolk"

Union Station, "Forest Fires"

Thanks also to the following print and audio anthologies, in which some of these poems have also appeared:

Alight: An Ebook of the Best Loved Poems from the 2013 Women of the World Poetry Slam, "The Type"

Chorus: A Literary Mixtape, "India Trio"

Courage: Daring Poems for Gutsy Girls, "Forest Fires," "Private Parts"

IndieFeed Performance Poetry podcast, "B," "Peacocks," "Hand-Me-Downs," "Brother," "Private Parts," "The Ladder"

Finally, many thanks to **Seth Godin** and **The Domino Project**, who published the poem **"B"** as a hardcover book in 2011.

Acknowledgments

This book exists thanks to the endless patience and hard work of Sophia Janowitz, Cristin O'Keefe Aptowicz, Jan Kawamura-Kay, Philip McCaffrey, Alex Kryger, Laura Lamb Brown-Lavoie, Derrick Brown, Anis Mojgani, the Serenbe Artists in Residency Program, and the editors and team at Write Bloody Publishing.

These poems exist thanks to the support and mentorship of the NYC Urbana Poetry Slam, the Bowery Poetry Club, all the poets of the New York City poetry community (but especially Taylor Mali, Cristin O'Keefe Aptowicz, Jeanann Verlee, and Rives), Frank Banton, Maureen Overall, Richard Kutner, Sheila Desmond, Providence poets (especially Franny Choi and Laura Lamb Brown-Lavoie), and the Pink Door Poetry Retreat.

These illustrations exist thanks to the insight and generosity of Sarah Wainwright, Joel Janowitz, Anne Lilly, Mark Ostow, Jan Kawamura-Kay, Jeffrey Kay, Marianna Pease, Andrew Bellisari, Marissa Grunes, Gloria O'Leary, Peter Tagiuri, and Mandy, Terry, Marina, and Rebecca Hopkins.

These adventures exist thanks to the guidance and encouragement of Project VOICE, Jeffrey Kay and the speakeasynyc YouTube channel, the TED community, Jacqueline Novogratz, Kelly Stoetzel, Chris Anderson, Seth Godin, Red Maxwell, Jean Oelwang, Anthony Veneziale, Carlos Andrés Gómez, Beau Sia, Rostam Afshinnekoo, Thomas Siefring, Lea Rangel-Ribeiro, Victor Ribeiro, the AT&T New Media Fellowship, Maggie Sarin, Arati Kaul, the Word Warriors of Kathmandu, the READ book group, the United Nations International School, Church Street School for Music and Art, and my students (at Hope, Classical, and all the other schools that I love).

This dream exists thanks to the faith and love of family (Kawamuras, Kays, Suzukis, Wainwrights, Janowitzs, Ferril-McCaffreys, Hsia-Schonzeits, Carson-Mordetskys), and friends (Sophia Janowitz, James Schonzeit, Tim Adams, Caroline Kissane, Tatiana Gellein, Phil Kaye, Emily Borromeo, Kayla Ringelheim, Alex Kryger, and all the Higher Keys).

This girl exists entirely because of Mom, Pop, and PK. Genji, June, Stewart, and Sylvia. And Lion and Blankie.

About the Author

Sarah Kay is a poet from New York City who was born in 1988. She has been performing spoken word poetry since she was fourteen years old. She was a featured poet on HBO's *Russell Simmons Presents Def Poetry Jam* in 2006, and that year she was also the youngest poet to compete in the National Poetry Slam. Since then, Sarah has shared her poetry on six of the seven continents and is currently yearning for Antarctica. She is perhaps best known for her talk at the 2011 TED conference, which garnered two standing ovations. Sarah holds a Masters Degree in The Art of Teaching from Brown University and an Honorary Doctorate in Humane Letters from Grinnell College. Her first book, *B*, was also illustrated by Sophia Janowitz and was ranked #1 Poetry Book on Amazon. Sarah is the founder of Project VOICE, an organization that uses spoken word poetry to encourage people to engage in creative self-expression in schools and communities around the world. She spends a lot of her time with a blanket and a stuffed animal lion. For more, see: kaysarahsera.com

About the Illustrator

Sophia Janowitz has created chickens out of bathmats and rubber gloves for the New York Philharmonic at Lincoln Center, chocolate buttons for a pop-up store in Boston, a poster for a musical premiering at the Jewish Refugees Museum in Shanghai, and a cardboard levitating house for a play premiering in New York City. She currently assists an editorial portrait photographer, tutors math, and draws every day. Some of her work can be seen at sophiajanowitz.com

If You Like Sarah Kay, Sarah Kay Likes . . .

The Year of No Mistakes
Cristin O'Keefe Aptowicz

Racing Hummingbirds
Jeanann Verlee

Songs From Under the River
Anis Mojgani

Floating, Brilliant, Gone
Franny Choi

Ceremony for the Choking Ghost
Karen Finneyfrock

The Last Time as We Are
Taylor Mali

Write Bloody Books

After the Witch Hunt — Megan Falley

Aim for the Head, Zombie Anthology — Rob Sturma, Editor

Amulet — Jason Bayani

Any Psalm You Want — Khary Jackson

Birthday Girl with Possum — Brendan Constantine

The Bones Below — Sierra DeMulder

Born in the Year of the Butterfly Knife — Derrick C. Brown

Bring Down the Chandeliers — Tara Hardy

Ceremony for the Choking Ghost — Karen Finneyfrock

Courage: Daring Poems for Gutsy Girls — Karen Finneyfrock, Mindy Nettifee & Rachel McKibbens, Editors

Dear Future Boyfriend — Cristin O'Keefe Aptowicz

Dive: The Life and Fight of Reba Tutt — Hannah Safren

Drunks and Other Poems of Recovery — Jack McCarthy

The Elephant Engine High Dive Revival anthology

Everything Is Everything — Cristin O'Keefe Aptowicz

The Feather Room — Anis Mojgani

Gentleman Practice — Buddy Wakefield

Glitter in the Blood: A Guide to Braver Writing — Mindy Nettifee

Good Grief — Stevie Edwards

The Good Things About America — Derrick Brown and Kevin Staniec, Editors

Hot Teen Slut — Cristin O'Keefe Aptowicz

I Love Science! — Shanny Jean Maney

I Love You is Back — Derrick C. Brown

The Importance of Being Ernest — Ernest Cline

In Search of Midnight — Mike McGee

The Incredible Sestina Anthology — Daniel Nester, Editor

Junkyard Ghost Revival anthology

Kissing Oscar Wilde — Jade Sylvan

The Last Time as We Are — Taylor Mali

Learn Then Burn — Tim Stafford and Derrick C. Brown, Editors

Learn Then Burn Teacher's Manual — Tim Stafford and Molly Meacham, Editors

Live For A Living — Buddy Wakefield

Love in a Time of Robot Apocalypse — David Perez

The Madness Vase — Andrea Gibson

The New Clean — Jon Sands

New Shoes On A Dead Horse — Sierra DeMulder

No Matter the Wreckage — Sarah Kay

Oh, Terrible Youth — Cristin O'Keefe Aptowicz

The Oregon Trail Is the Oregon Trail — Gregory Sherl

Over the Anvil We Stretch — Anis Mojgani

Pole Dancing to Gospel Hymns — Andrea Gibson

Racing Hummingbirds — Jeanann Verlee

Rise of the Trust Fall — Mindy Nettifee

Scandalabra — Derrick C. Brown

Slow Dance With Sasquatch — Jeremy Radin

The Smell of Good Mud — Lauren Zuniga

Songs from Under the River — Anis Mojgani

Spiking the Sucker Punch — Robbie Q. Telfer

Strange Light — Derrick C. Brown

These Are The Breaks — Idris Goodwin

Time Bomb Snooze Alarm — Bucky Sinister

The Undisputed Greatest Writer of All Time — Beau Sia

What Learning Leaves — Taylor Mali

What the Night Demands — Miles Walser

Working Class Represent — Cristin O'Keefe Aptowicz

Write About An Empty Birdcage — Elaina Ellis

Yarmulkes & Fitted Caps — Aaron Levy Samuels

The Year of No Mistakes — Cristin O'Keefe Aptowicz

Yesterday Won't Goodbye — Brian S. Ellis